DARE WE HOPE?

Pumla Gobodo-Madikizela

*'If memory is used to rekindle old hatreds, it will lead
us back to continuing hatred and conflict.
But if memory is used to rebuild, or to begin new
relationships, that is where hope lies.'*

Some of these articles have appeared in different versions
in earlier publications.

Tafelberg
an imprint of NB Publishers
a division of Media24 Boeke (Pty) Ltd
40 Heerengracht, Cape Town 8001

Text © Pumla Gobodo-Madikizela (2014)

Editor: Riaan de Villiers
Book design by Firelight Studio
Cover photo by Sonia Small
Cover design by Michiel Botha
Set in Minion Pro 10.5 pt

Printed and bound by Paarl Media Paarl,
Jan van Riebeeck Drive, Paarl, South Africa
First edition, first impression 2014

ISBN: 978-0-624-06863-1
ISBN (epub): 978-0-624-06864-8
ISBN (mobi): 978-0-624-06865-5

For my father, in memoriam …

TABLE OF CONTENTS

FOREWORD

Tonight I am reaching out to every single South African, black and white, from the very depths of my being. A white man, full of prejudice and hate, came to our country and committed a deed so foul that our whole nation now teeters on the brink of disaster. A white woman, of Afrikaner origin, risked her life so that we may know, and bring to justice, this assassin [...] This is a watershed moment for all of us. Our decisions and actions will determine whether we use our pain, our grief, and our outrage to move forward to what is the only lasting solution for our country.

NELSON MANDELA, 10 APRIL 1993

IN APRIL 1993, the former commander of the armed wing of the African National Congress (ANC), Chris Hani, was gunned down in the driveway of his home in a multiracial suburb in Boksburg, a city in the Gauteng province of South Africa. One of Hani's neighbours, a white woman, took the registration number of the assassin's car as he fled from the scene of the crime. She called the police, and Hani's killer was arrested shortly after the incident.

Amidst fears that the country would erupt into violence, Nelson Mandela appeared on prime time national television on the day of Hani's assassination to call for calm. In the minds of many black South Africans, Chris Hani epitomised the ultimate fighter for the struggle for freedom against the white apartheid government. If Nelson Mandela in prison was the embodiment of the vision for freedom, Chris Hani, as the commander of the military wing of the ANC, Umkhonto weSizwe (literally 'the Spear of the Nation'), kept that vision alive with its concrete expression. Hani returned to South Africa after the unbanning of the ANC when all exiled anti-apartheid activists were granted indemnity shortly after the release of Nelson Mandela in February 1990. In 1993, the political negotiations for a multiparty democracy were in progress, and Hani's assassination was seen as a ploy by the white right wing to derail the negotiations process. In the end, however, it was a historical turning point. The negotiations, which had been experiencing setbacks, moved forward with greater resolve, leading to a decision to hold South Africa's first all-race elections in April the following year.

Nelson Mandela was not yet president when he addressed the nation to calm emotions that were threatening to explode. Yet he was already being presidential, setting the tone for the kind of leadership that South Africa needed. For Mandela then, the critical moment of Hani's death was at once a moment of grief and a call reminding the nation of the vision of peaceful freedom, an opportunity for dialogue about the past that divided us, and an invitation to pursue the transformation of our future. South Africans heeded the call and moved forward to embrace Mandela's quest to leave the divisions of the past behind in order to build a new country. The foundation for this was his vision that connection between former enemies was better than rekindling old hatred. Throughout his journey to restore peace in South Africa, Mandela used moments of rupture as opportunities to break open the possibility for collective reflection and connection. He introduced a new language that transformed the narrative of violence in South Africa, and for the first time, there was a strong sense of social solidarity that united South Africans across racial lines and instilled national pride.

Only a few months after the passing of Nelson Mandela in December 2013, the need to return to his vision remains clear. The mass shooting of striking mineworkers by members of the South African Police Service in Marikana, the ongoing strike by mineworkers demanding the dignity of salaries commensurate with the work they do for the Lonmin platinum mining companies, the violent demonstrations against poor service delivery in black township communities across South Africa, and the massive corruption at the highest level of government are examples of the kind of 'watershed moment' that Nelson Mandela refers to in the quote above. As I write this introduction, I have just participated in a special Commission set up to investigate problems of policing in Khayelitsha as one of expert witnesses called to share their insights on a range of issues related to policing and what has been termed 'vigilante violence' in Khayelitsha. Khayelitsha is not the only township in the Cape Town region that has experienced a rising tide of violence, where even young children have been caught up in various ways, not least the insidious trauma of witnessing violence and murder regularly. South Africa is a troubled country. As we respond with outrage to the events around the country that are threatening to shatter Mandela's legacy, we remember his call 'to use our pain, our grief, and our outrage' to reconnect with our common humanity – instead of becoming stuck in despair, 'to move forward' and find meaning and inspiration in the richness of the lessons he left behind.

The hope that Nelson Mandela inspired was grounded in the quest for us to establish a richer sense of our identity as human beings, connected to others in the human community. He expanded the horizons of what is possible in human relationships by spearheading, as part of the political negotiations, a process of dialogue, fostering the capacity for connecting with others – even others who are former enemies – in order to confront and heal a past characterised by moral corruption and widespread violations of human rights. Twenty years ago, Nelson Mandela, leading his comrades and compatriots with moral stature, brought forth the birth of hope in our country. We need a dialogue among all South Africans – 'united in our diversity' – on how we might continue investing in our citizenship a dedication to raising our voices and taking action where we can in order to take on the challenges facing our country.

Pumla Gobodo-Madikizela

Cape Town, May 2014

REMEMBRANCE AND RECONCILIATION

'The heart of forgiveness does not necessarily lie in loving those around us (it definitely does not lie in hating them either). The spirit of forgiveness lies in the search – not for the things that separate us – but for something common among us as fellow human beings, the compassion and empathy that binds our human identity.'

1. Facing the truth in South Africa

THE WASHINGTON POST, 1 NOVEMBER 1998

Serving on South Africa's Truth and Reconciliation Commission as a coordinator of the public hearings in the Western Cape gave me an opportunity to witness its limitations and achievements at first hand. When, in late 1998, the commission released its final report, I felt the public reactions confirmed that the task of dealing with our past had still not been concluded.

THE LONG-AWAITED FINAL report of South Africa's Truth and Reconciliation Commission (TRC), which was released last week, will lay nothing to rest. It appears at a time when the South African public has tired of the commission, and become sceptical about its benefits. White people are increasingly negative about everything – the economy, crime, affirmative action, and a government run by a cabinet that is mainly black.

These negative attitudes are a screen against confronting the reality of their contribution to apartheid, a system that oppressed the majority of South Africans for the enrichment of a few, and their status as beneficiaries of its privileges. Perpetrators continue to struggle with the effects of public shaming and of being exposed as the doers of evil deeds.

Some victims are also unhappy. They have not seen any benefit from having come forward to the commission to share their stories of anguish. Their hopes were wearing thin until the first reparation payments were made recently to a few victims, a process seen as too little, too late.

The TRC has forced white people to reckon with their role as bystanders and beneficiaries of apartheid privilege. Many of them have refused to face this truth, which threatens their sense of humanity. Instead, they have been excessively critical of the post-apartheid government and its efforts towards transformation, which they regard as a threat to the privileges they were used to under apartheid.

The struggle by perpetrators of apartheid atrocities is a struggle to find meaning in their past. Unlike their political opponents – those who fought in the liberation movement, and are able to salvage some sense of meaning from the acts of violence – there are few threads of meaning to link apartheid perpetrators to the past. Exposed in shame through the TRC's work, perpetrators often tried to minimise the extent of their involvement in atrocities by continuing to lie, as if they would not have to tell the whole truth and could get away with murder once again, as they were used to, with denial and solidarity in the lie.

Victims were unhappy because they felt the TRC had abandoned them and did not fulfil the promises it had made. The commission addressed some of their emotional needs arising out of traumatic memory, but they had to return to the reality of their unchanged economic situation. Putting a face to the perpetrators who had brought them years of anguish, and knowing the facts about how it happened, removed some of the emotional burden they had carried over the years, but this did not improve their life circumstances.

Very few people will appreciate the TRC's most valuable achievements. Perhaps the most valuable is its attempt to answer the question: how can a country move forward from a history of oppression and violence without destroying itself with revenge?

It is not surprising that attitudes to the TRC are critical. It has been a pain-filled process for everyone, and people are still dealing with bitterness, guilt, disappointment, anger and grief. But the report presented last Thursday should be seen as part of dealing with the past and of seeking reconciliation, even if such reconciliation will not come in this generation.

While some victims have been unhappy about having come forward with their stories, many others feel an incredible sense of validation after having testified at the public hearings. For these victims, nothing was more affirming than an opportunity to break the silence about the brutality they had experienced during the apartheid years.

The TRC allowed some victims and survivors to encounter their perpetrators in ways that would not have been possible in a court of law. Here lies one of its successes: the requests for forgiveness made by some perpetrators, and the granting of forgiveness by victims and survivors who are the primary generation of sufferers of atrocities, are unprecedented in the history of atrocities in the 20th century. Its greatest success is the fact that South Africa has not plunged into a spiral of violence and revenge.

2. The roots of Afrikaner rage

New York Times, 10 January 2003

In October 2002 a bomb blast in Soweto destroyed railway lines and a mosque, and killed a young woman in her sleep. A right-wing group called 'Die Boeremag' (The Afrikaner Force) claimed responsibility, declaring it seeking revenge for attacks on Afrikaner farmers; demanded that Boeremag members be released from prison; and threatened further attacks. This prompted me to reflect on the position of Afrikaners in South Africa, who also have a long and bitter history of struggle. At the same time, the past had taught me that revenge is a heavy burden to carry.[1]

'THESE WERE PLACES black people were forbidden to go,' says my mother as we approach a restaurant in an upmarket Cape Town shopping mall. 'And now we can come to the same places as whites, walk into a café, and pay the same money – just like that.'

For some white South Africans, mingling with blacks in urban malls is a welcome change from the racial isolation of the past. Some are simply resigned to this post-apartheid reality, and merely tolerate the presence of black people in these places. But for others, the appearance of black faces in spaces that were previously reserved for whites is seen as an invasion of what belongs to them – things they worked so hard to build, their pride, their fatherland. This has evoked bitterness, and unleashed their wrath and violent outrage.

---

[1]   See 'Boeremag Treason Trial Timeline', South African History Online, http://www.sahistory.org.za/topic/boeremag-treason-trial-timeline; B Ndaba and T Wa Sepotokele, 'Soweto residents: "We're still living in fear"', *Independent Online,* 6 November 2002; N Mulder, 'We planted the bombs', *Beeld,* 10 November 2002; 'Right-wing group claims Soweto blasts', *BBC News,* 11 November 2002; 'S African whites face treason trial', *BBC News,* 3 June 2003.

Having been a child and an adult under apartheid, and having grown up in a family and community of dispossessed and disenfranchised adults, I can understand their anger. For the sake of the nation's future peace and unity, I hope everyone concerned will consider its sources.

Seeds of hatred continue to fester among Afrikaners who feel that the new democracy in South Africa and the freedoms enjoyed by blacks have robbed them of their heritage. While the buzzword in South Africa has been 'reconciliation', and while the rest of the world has praised the political transition in this country as a miracle, and a civil war that didn't happen, some Afrikaners feel marginalised by a process that has ended decades of legalised oppression of blacks by a white minority government. They hate the power that the democratic changes have bestowed on a black government. They have lashed out in vengeance with a bombing spree that has President Thabo Mbeki's government seizing arms caches and arresting suspects in the hope of destroying a network of right-wing militants.

The cry of the extreme right-wingers is for an '*eie staat*' (our own state), what their forefathers fought for, and what was later written into apartheid laws. In 1952, the then prime minister, Dr DF Malan, responded to the leaders of the African National Congress and the South African Indian Congress, who had jointly led the Defiance Campaign in June that year, by writing: 'The road to peace and goodwill lies in giving each group the opportunity of developing its ambitions and capacities in its own area, or within its own community on its own lines, in the service of its own people.'

Then, those words were intended to seal the fate of black people, who would be evicted from their homes and banished to nominally independent 'homelands'. Now, under a black government, the concept of an *eie staat*, for which Afrikaners fought and died under British rule, and which served them when they were in power, is still being invoked.

Some see the rising tide of discontent among Afrikaners as evidence of racist attitudes that won't go away. This may be so. But we must also consider the bitter memories that have been unleashed by the transfer of power to a black government. Most Afrikaners carry in their consciousness the spirit of survival; there is always an 'other' against whom the volk must be protected. They suffered serious loss and humiliation in their war with the British, the Anglo-Boer War.

In that conflict, which began in 1899, British troops destroyed thousands of Boer farms, blew up homesteads, and set land and cattle ablaze. Thousands of Afrikaner women, children and elderly men were sent to internment camps, where many died from disease and cold. Official estimates place the number of Afrikaners who perished in British camps at 20 000 to 27 000. In 1902, home-less and humiliated, the Afrikaners lost their fight against British domination.

Former president PW Botha, raised when memories of that war were fresh, was the father of apartheid's 'total strategy' against opponents of the South African state in the worst period of apartheid violence, the 1980s. Many Afrikaners were brought up to believe that fighting for their survival was the very essence of their identity. It will take something other than force to break the cycle of hatred and the desire for vengeful violence.

Former president FW de Klerk, speaking about reconciliation in 1997, referred to the 'devastation' the British had visited upon the Afrikaners. 'It deprived us of our hard-won right to rule ourselves,' he said. 'But somehow or other, we have succeeded in putting most of this bitterness behind us.'

After the British, there was another enemy. De Klerk apologised to South Africans who were oppressed by apartheid laws, 'in a spirit of true repentance'. Yet the ghosts of the past have not been laid to rest, at least not completely. The dialogue that was begun by the Truth and Reconciliation Commission must continue in order to forge and strengthen a spirit of compromise and tolerance. Acknowledging the loss that Afrikaners feel would be a start.

The task of picking up the pieces of a society shattered by violence is not easy. My mother, who grew up in rural KwaZulu-Natal, remembers the loss of her family's land, and witnessed the humiliation of a father who had to seek work in that faraway place which black people called Gauteng, 'the place of gold'. She and my father were married in Cape Town in 1951, the year in which the apartheid government passed more than 70 oppressive laws. She, like many black people I know, has every reason to remember with bitterness, and to harbour a desire for revenge. But she prefers to live without that burden.

3. The TRC: unfinished business

THISDAY, 4 MARCH 2004

The Truth and Reconciliation Commission granted the apartheid-era security policeman Gideon Nieuwoudt amnesty for his role in the deaths of the student activists Siphiwe Mthimkhulu and Topsy Mdaka, but refused him amnesty in respect of the deaths of the Motherwell Four. Following this, Nieuwoudt and three other security policemen were arrested on charges of murder. Some commentators argued against their prosecution on the grounds that the possible implication of politicians or senior government officials in the course of the trial could hamper national reconciliation. This prompted me to re-examine the role of amnesty as well as prosecution in the course of the reconciliation process.[2]

---

[2]   Nieuwoudt – a member of the Port Elizabeth Security Branch between 1977 and 1989 – sought amnesty in respect of the kidnapping and killing of Siphiwe Mthimkulu and Topsy Madaka in April 1982; the kidnapping and death of the 'PEBCO Three' in May 1985; the Motherwell car bombing which killed four people in December 1989; the assaults on the Black Consciousness leader Steve Biko and his friend Peter Jones in September 1977; and an assault on the activist Mkhuseli Jack in August 1985. He was refused amnesty in respect of Biko, but never prosecuted; granted amnesty in respect of Mthimkhulu and Mdaka; and refused amnesty in respect of the PEBCO Three and the Motherwell bombing. Following this, he and two other security policemen, Marthinus Ras and Wybrandt du Toit, were convicted of murder in respect of the Motherwell bombings and given lengthy prison sentences, but they won a court order setting aside the TRC's original decision and instructing it to stage a new amnesty hearing. Nieuwoudt and another former security policeman, Johannes 'Sakkie' van Zyl, were also charged with murder in respect of the PEBCO Three. Out on bail, Nieuwoudt was waiting for the outcome of the renewed amnesty application when he died of cancer in August 2005. In decisions announced four months later, the special committee pardoned Ras and Du Toit, but again turned down Nieuwoudt's application on the grounds that he had not disclosed all the facts related to the incident. See *Mail & Guardian*, 'Nieuwoudt to apply for amnesty', 22 March 2004, http://mg.co.za/article/2004-03-22-nieuwoudt-to-apply-for-amnesty/; 'No reprieve for Gideon Nieuwoudt', 1 July 2005, http://mg.co.za/article/2005-07-01-no-reprieve-for-gideon-nieuwoudt; 'Former apartheid cop Gideon Nieuwoudt dies', 20 August 2005, http://mg.co.za/article/2005-08-20-former-apartheidcop-gideon-nieuwoudt-dies; 'Committee refuses amnesty for Nieuwoudt', 22 December 2005, http://mg.co.za/article/2005-12-22-committee-refuses-amnesty-for-nieuwoudt.

SPEAKING VERY SOFTLY, her voice strained by illness and years of struggle searching for the truth about the whereabouts of her son's remains, Joyce Mthimkhulu is tired. Her son Siphiwe was detained, tortured and poisoned by the apartheid security police in the Eastern Cape. He disappeared after suing the state for gross abuse and attempted murder. His body was never found.

When she appeared at a public hearing of the Truth and Reconciliation Commission (TRC), she raised in her hands the only remains she has of her son: the mass of hair that fell out as a result of thallium poisoning. She had kept her son's hair, she said, in the hope that one day she might be able to bury it with his remains. She is still waiting.

The man whom Joyce Mthimkhulu believes holds the key to that truth, Gideon Nieuwoudt, testified before the TRC that her son's body had been burnt, and his ashes scattered in the Fish River. Nieuwoudt was granted amnesty for the murder of Siphiwe and his companion, Topsy Madaka, but was denied amnesty due to his lack of candour about his and his unit's role in the PEBCO Three and Motherwell Bombing incidents. Now Nieuwoudt has been arrested by the Scorpions, and released on bail. He has a second chance to disclose the full details of the human rights abuses for which he admitted responsibility before the TRC, including, according to Joyce Mthimkhulu, information on where Siphiwe's remains are buried.

Some believe the arrest of Nieuwoudt and his former colleagues who did not apply for amnesty, or were denied amnesty, may 'hamper reconciliation'. The vigorous prosecution of Nieuwoudt and his ilk, they suggest, will throw the reconciliation agenda into chaos because of the possible disclosure of the names of high-ranking officials in the former apartheid government. But are such disclosures not the very essence of reconciliation? Was it not this promise of the truth that encouraged victims and survivors to embrace the idea of reconciliation, lending legitimacy to the 'justice' of the quasi-legal process of the TRC?

Nieuwoudt, who is out on bail until June when his court hearing is scheduled to resume, no doubt enjoys hearing remarks about the potential 'hampering' of reconciliation if his prosecution goes ahead. A Cape Town newspaper recently quoted him as saying that continuing his trial would show that the government was not serious about reconciliation.

Rather than encourage Nieuwoudt and others to use the commitment to reconciliation as a form of ransom, ways of moving them towards contrition and some measure of genuine regret for their deeds should be considered. These prosecutions, as I see them, will contribute to South Africa's dealing with the unfinished business of the TRC – unfinished because of the gaping void left by undisclosed truth. They lead us towards the road of moral humanity that lies ahead on our journey of reconciliation. Nieuwoudt and others like him should rise to the challenge of honouring victims and their families, and to be honourable. Allowing them to go free at this point would not only reward them, but would also prevent any corresponding compensation for victims, who were granted a mere R30 000 for reparations.

Joyce Mthimkhulu has not received the reparations promised by the president in April last year. She says that when she phoned the justice department to find out why her payment was delayed, she was informed that the department had been going through the claims in alphabetical order. 'What does the alphabet have to do with it?' she asks with exasperation. 'Why should our pain be reduced to the way the alphabet is constructed?' She and her husband are waiting for the money not out of greed, she says, but because they need it to pay their medical bills. Her husband suffered a stroke that affected his speech, and she has had a series of health problems.

Nieuwoudt has visited her home to apologise. His arrogance and contempt for the process of reconciliation is clearly evident in a documentary by Mark Kaplan entitled 'Between Joyce and Remembrance'. Nieuwoudt tells Joyce and her husband that he, like them, is a Christian. It's now time to forgive, forget the past and reconcile. 'I have done my duty,' he says, referring to the 'duty' of coming to their home to ask their forgiveness. In the same film, Siphiwe's only surviving son, S'khumbuzo, asks how he can be expected to forgive when he has not been able to find his father's body. 'They didn't even leave a single bone,' he says.

In the past, victims knew that the legal route was no antidote for crimes committed by the security police. Gross human rights abuses were impervious to the normal principles of law – as if one could call the justice system of the past 'normal'. The process of justice today should not remind victims of their marginalised status in the past. Saving Nieuwoudt from prosecution will vindicate him, and add to the victims' pain.

A programme of rewarding perpetrators, either through presidential pardon or other kinds of amnesty, should follow a clear vision guided by the spirit of the goals set out in the Promotion of National Unity and Reconciliation Act that governed the TRC: those who confess fully, and those who have demonstrated a dedication to national reconciliation, should be considered for political pardon.

The state's commitment to pursue the prosecution of perpetrators of human rights abuses who were refused amnesty for specific crimes, and those who did not apply for amnesty, is a sign that the government takes reconciliation seriously. Far from threatening reconciliation, those prosecutions are essential for holding perpetrators accountable, and therefore a positive element of reconciliation.

If former senior apartheid leaders share in the ideal of healing and reconciliation for our country, their being named in public, if it happens, should be valued as an important contribution to the country's post-apartheid transition. This would elevate victims' suffering from being mere footnotes in the story of South Africa's reconciliation process.

4. The politics of revenge will fail

THISDAY, 19 MAY 2004

In May 2004, the American broadcaster CBS aired images of the torture and abuse of prisoners in the Abu Ghraib prison at the hands of American military personnel and government officials. At that time, I was on a lecture tour of the United States, speaking about my book on my experiences at the Truth and Reconciliation Commission. The events at Abu Ghraib bore an uncanny resemblance to the forms of torture described by victims of apartheid, and I became troubled by the grammar of violence with which the American government responded.

SEVERAL WEEKS AGO I was interviewed on a live show on American National Public Radio (NPR). The occasion was the launch of the paperback edition of my book *A Human Being Died That Night*,[3] and the radio discussion included the third democratic elections since the ANC's 1994 victory; the Truth and Reconciliation Commission (TRC); how South Africa moved on after the bloody conflict of the past, and some of the challenges it faces now; and forgiveness and reconciliation.

At some point in my conversation with the host, the lines were opened to allow listeners to share their views. One of the callers, an Irish-American woman, questioned the significance of the TRC in the lives of blacks in South Africa. 'How can they [black people] allow this thing to happen?' she asked. She went on to express her discontent with current discussions in Northern Ireland about the possibility of introducing a process similar to the TRC.

---

[3]   Pumla Goboda-Madikizela, *A Human Being Died That Night: A South African Story of Forgiveness*, Boston: Houghton Mifflin, 2003.

She made it clear that she was opposed to any idea that would fall short of punishing the British for the years of pain and anguish they had caused in Northern Ireland. She cited 'Bloody Sunday', an incident in which Catholic civilians involved in a peaceful march against detention without trial were killed by British troops – an equivalent of the Sharpeville Massacre – as an example of the evils of the British: 'I want the British to suffer for what they did to us,' she said. Her anger on air was palpable.

Earlier that day I had lunch with Alex Boraine, former chair of the TRC, in Lower Manhattan, reflecting with a sense of pride on the kind of leadership we have been privileged to have as South Africans, from Nelson Mandela, to Archbishop Tutu, to FW de Klerk and to Thabo Mbeki, and on the achievements of our country: how we got it right, managing to quell the instinct for revenge, even as we continue to struggle with many serious social and economic problems.

At a time when the unfolding story of the 21st century is a pursuit for vengeance through ruthless murder and bloody massacres, violent wars conducted with weapons of mass destruction, peace deals between former enemies collapsing into cycles of bloody conflict, where heads of states are not afraid to publicly declare their desire to target other leaders and to 'eliminate' them, one feels proud to be a South African.

South Africa today serves as a reminder of how political leaders can transcend hatred and embody the shared goals of the spirit of national unity. It helps to take a look back and see just how far we have come. The fight for freedom from oppressive laws and for basic human rights, and the government's severe measures to suppress opposition, ushered in a ferocious struggle between government on the one hand and the liberation movement and the majority of South Africans on the other, which led to a venomous style of engagement that left many dead. The government deemed all who fought for freedom 'terrorists' who had to be eliminated.

That is not too long ago, which is why it is remarkable that today the enemies who sought to destroy one another sit on the same side in parliament sharing power as compatriots, and that South Africa is a more tolerant and inclusive society. That South Africa is the miracle that the world sees it to be is largely due to the millions of survivors of apartheid oppression who have chosen not to stoop to the vengeful patterns of history. Some call it reconciliation, others a generosity of spirit and an ability to forgive. But I think it is all these, plus the 'soft vengeance' of voting power.

The United States today is a reminder of what South Africa was, and how those in power can breed hatred that produces cycles of violence that go on, and on, and on. When I was in New York, the news was dominated by questions to the Bush administration about the detention without trial of prisoners in Guantánamo Bay, and the infringements of American citizens' rights in the wake of the 'war against terror'. Today, America has to face the consequences of choosing the path of making its enemies suffer; America has become that which it loathes. It is a small step from fighting evil to becoming evil.

The wish to inflict suffering means that one has to get into the skin of the perpetrator, become like him, and often exceed the brutality of what is being avenged. American soldiers jubilantly displayed in front of TV cameras the dead bodies of Saddam Hussein's sons, and we have watched in the news the shocking pictures of decapitated Iraqi children and dead women – casualties of the war, collateral damage they call them. If we accept these excesses in what the Bush administration calls the fight against terrorism, will our intellectual sensibilities allow us to condemn the Iraqis who paraded the charred and mutilated corpses of four

Americans in the streets of Fallujah? Can we in all honesty join Senator McCain and other leaders in the US administration in calling the horrific beheading of an American citizen to avenge the torture of Iraqi prisoners in Abu Ghraib 'barbaric', without condemning the very act that unleashed this cycle of vengeance?

In the 'War on Terror', the tables have turned, and the victim has moved from victor to perpetrator. There is no surprise in the torture by American prison guards at Abu Ghraib. The language of hatred, the lexicon of dehumanisation and torture has been part and parcel of this war. The prison guards felt, rightly, that there could be nothing wrong with abusing Iraqi prisoners, 'enemies of freedom', in front of cameras. They have taken the cue from their leaders. President Bush wants the world to believe that the Abu Ghraib images represent actions that are un-American, that the torture is the work of a few bad apples. Well then, it is time to seek alternatives to this destructive war in order to prevent future perverse acts.

America has become our past. We in South Africa are familiar with leaders who encouraged foot soldiers to make the state's enemies suffer, and then when the moment of reckoning came, told the world that the barbaric acts were aberrant, committed by a few individuals who were inspired not by the noble goals of the government, but by their own potential for evil. This is a good time for the Bush administration to reflect on the escalating bloody violence of this war, and to change course. Revenge – making one's enemies suffer – is not the right path. Choosing to respond to violence by engaging one's enemy in dialogue is a risk, but as we know in South Africa, it is one worth taking. That is the lesson South Africa offers the world.

5. We must restore the human spirit

ThisDay, June 2004

Early in 2003, as part of my American lecture tour about my book A
Human Being Died That Night, *I addressed a gathering in the Los
Angeles Public Library.[4] An extraordinary encounter with a fellow
South African later prompted me to write this article.*

THE WOMAN IN the audience raised her hand and waved it fran-
tically. It was early 2003, and I had just given a lecture at the Los
Angeles public library during my American book tour. The reporter
from the *LA Weekly* who was chairing the event announced that
she was going to take the last question, and I pointed at the woman
who seemed desperate for a chance to speak.

'I am an Afrikaner,' she said. 'I read your book last night, and
feel an incredible need to speak right now.' She went on to explain
that she had come to the United States to pursue postgraduate
studies in international relations; she had been burdened with guilt
for having benefited from apartheid, and reading the book had
stirred her deeply. Her voice trembled as she continued: 'When I
complete my degree, I want to return home to South Africa and
pay back in whatever way I can. More than anything,' she said, now
weeping visibly, 'I want to ask for forgiveness for having benefited
from a system that destroyed so many lives.'

The woman was crying and trying to speak, and she cast a
lonely figure; she had exposed herself and made herself vulnerable.
She had told her deepest truth in public. I took a few steps forward
and extended my hand to reach out to her from the edge of the

---

[4] For a report on this lecture, see L Steinman, 'The Truth Shall Set You Free:
Pumla Gobodo-Madikizela on the evils of apartheid and finding forgiveness', *LA
Weekly*, 31 January 2003.

stage. She came towards me, still sobbing. There was stillness in the packed auditorium. You could have heard a pin drop. As we embraced, the audience applauded.

Listening to the long applause, and remembering the deep silence in the large hall when she spoke earlier, it was clear to me that the applause was not simply a response of approval. The spontaneous gesture between us had stirred something in the mainly white American audience. Two people from different sides of history in a country that had almost descended into civil war, coming together in a spontaneous embrace after this 'conversation' about the past. It was a story that resonated with the audience longing for a resolution of their own past, not least the as-yet-unacknowledged trauma of slavery that continues to haunt both white and black Americans.

Not all Afrikaners, or white South Africans for that matter, are willing or able to engage privately or publicly in the way this woman did. Seeds of hatred continue to fester among many whites, who feel that the new democracy in South Africa and the freedoms enjoyed by blacks have robbed them of their heritage. Some whites feel marginalised by the end of the legalised oppression of blacks with the fall of the apartheid government. They resent the power that the democratic changes have bestowed on a black-led government and their own perceived loss of power. A far-right group of Afrikaners has even lashed out in vengeance in the past through bombing sprees.

Discontent among whites has sometimes been seen as evidence of continuing racism, and this might be the case. But we also must consider the bitter memories that have been unleashed by the transfer of power to the democratic government. Some Afrikaners carry with them the awareness of how the *volk* (the Afrikaner people) had to fight to maintain the spirit of survival; they had to protect themselves from the 'other' that threatened their wellbeing. Notably, they suffered serious loss and humiliation in their war with the British.

Many Afrikaners were brought up to believe that fighting for their survival was the very essence of their identity. Former president FW de Klerk, speaking about reconciliation in 1997, referred to the loss of power the Afrikaners experienced as a result of their war with the British. 'It deprived us of our hard-won right to rule ourselves,' he said. 'But somehow or other, we have succeeded in putting most of this bitterness behind us.'

Democracy has been with us for ten years now. Yet the ghosts of the past have not been laid to rest, at least not completely. It will take something other than simple conciliatory words from leaders to break the cycle of hatred. In addition to creating economic equality, the dialogue that was begun by the Truth and Reconciliation Commission must continue, so that we are able to forge and strengthen a spirit of compromise and tolerance in our society.

Listening to one another and acknowledging the experience of loss on both sides would be a start. The task of picking up the pieces of a society shattered by violence is not easy. It needs patience. Our humanity is strongest when we are focused on that which unites us as human beings: compassion, and an ethos of care for one another, rather than giving in to fear and suspicion.

My mother experienced some of the injustices of apartheid as she grew up in rural KwaZulu-Natal: her family lost their land; they witnessed the humiliation of her father, who had to seek work in faraway Gauteng; and she and my father were married in Cape Town in 1951, the year in which more than 70 oppressive laws were passed by the apartheid government. They endured every single one of those laws. My mother, and many black people I know, have every reason to remember those experiences with bitterness, and could harbour a desire for revenge. But they prefer to live without that burden.

Reconciliation cannot be condensed into a quick-fix project, one that has to take place within a prescribed space of time. It needs work, on a personal and public level. Perhaps the most enduring effects of totalitarian rule and the systematic oppression under apartheid cannot be measured in terms of numbers of the dead, but in immeasurable losses of the human spirit. That is what has to be restored.

How does this society restore its humane fabric in the aftermath of a horrific past? By understanding why some white people feel a sense of loss in the new South Africa; by understanding why the liberation movement was necessary, and why human rights abuses were committed in the process. By having a dialogue about why so many white people supported apartheid at a time when the international community was issuing calls for its dismantling.

Was the refusal to take a stand against apartheid a reflection of an inherently evil characteristic among white voters? Did the majority of whites fail to apply their best judgment because the effects of apartheid on the oppressed were not sufficiently understood, because of the effectiveness of the propaganda, or because of the psychological denial that so often occurs in totalitarian regimes?

How should present society judge white compatriots who, by virtue of supporting apartheid, were therefore its public face? Do we judge them with the same revulsion as we judge the system which they supported? Or do we reserve such judgment for the 'evil' ones who executed apartheid's opponents? How do white people who supported apartheid reflect on the past? Do they acknowledge any wrongdoing? Are they remorseful? And when they acknowledge wrongdoing and show remorse, what should our response be? Should we reject their apology and continue to punish them with our hatred? Or should we extend our compassion, and invite them to journey with us on the road of moral humanity?

Ordinary people, under certain circumstances, are capable of far greater evil than we could have imagined. But so are we capable of far greater virtue than we might have thought. To restore the human spirit in our society, to open the door to the possibility of transformation, we must be led by the compassion that unites us as human beings. That road to regaining our humanity, the true freedom from the 'bondage of fear', that Alan Paton spoke about so prophetically in his book *Cry the Beloved Country*, we will reach only through consistent dialogue, with one another, about our pasts.

The woman in Los Angeles spoke the truth of her heart. It was a simple communication of what she felt. We reached out to each other and shared a common idiom of humanity as South Africans, regretting our past, wishing to mend it.

When I shared this story at an event hosted by Njabulo Ndebele, vice-chancellor of the University of Cape Town, he used a metaphor that best captures how this dialogue can be understood: making public spaces intimate. It is in these small steps, in the small spaces where we are, that we will be able to make a difference in our relationships and in our society. The challenge is to have the courage to start. To acknowledge. If memory is used to rekindle old hatreds, it will lead us back to continuing hatred and conflict. But if memory is used to rebuild, or to begin new relationships, that is where hope lies.

6. What we can learn from Nieuwoudt and De Kock

THISDAY, 4 AUGUST 2004

When, in July 2004, Eugene de Kock, incarcerated former commander of the notorious apartheid-era police counter-insurgency unit stationed at Vlakplaas, testified at Gideon Nieuwoudt's second amnesty hearing, he apologised for his own involvement in the Motherwell car bombing to the families of the four victims. By contrast, Nieuwoudt presented evidence that he was suffering from post-traumatic stress disorder, which may have affected his previous evidence. It occurred to me that the difference between the two perpetrators' responses to the past holds the key to our nation's healing.[5]

EUGENE DE KOCK and Gideon Nieuwoudt, at once different and similar, have again entered the public discourse. These two crusaders for the apartheid state both snuffed out the lives of those who fought, in ways violent and non-violent, to bring us the democracy that we so proudly embrace today. But there is something that we miss in portraying these two men as 'exceptional', as 'rogues'.

They, like many who kept the apartheid government in power, believed in the political order of the day. Moreover, De Kock and Nieuwoudt were characteristic of the majority of white voters during the apartheid years. They may individually represent the ruthlessness of that deadly era, when state enemies were 'removed from society', but many white families during the apartheid years collectively participated in the conscription of their sons into the

---

[5] IOLnews, 'Nieuwoudt showed malicious intent – De Kock', 19 July 2004, http://www.iol.co.za/news/south-africa/nieuwoudt-showed-malicious-intent-de-kock-1.217574#.UxAheIWj0ns.

army to fight openly in the black townships the war that De Kock and Nieuwoudt were fighting in the shadows.

The apartheid laws might have been conceived and debated in political and religious corridors of power, but their implementation was not hidden from view; black people were openly pushed away from any semblance of a shot at equal opportunity. White people, with a few exceptions, were happy to maintain the status quo and to continue enjoying the privileges that De Kock and Nieuwoudt fought to protect. I bring this up not to evoke white guilt, but to remind ourselves that in order for our reconciliation agenda to be effective, and to heal the wounds of the past, we must recognise our collective role in it. The success of an evil political system like apartheid, like Nazism, like the genocide of the Tutsis in Rwanda, does not reside in one or two individuals.

The cry 'Never, and never again' will have meaningful significance only when we begin to realise that we would probably have been just like any ordinary South African who knowingly or inadvertently supported apartheid, a system that was declared a crime against humanity by the international community – as bystanders, beneficiaries, collaborators, or morally culpable in some other way.

Good and evil exist in all of us. Portraying De Kock and his ilk as the villains who should 'hang' for the sins of the past allows us to believe that we are morally superior. But, sadly, reality does not allow that kind of fantasy. Denouncing the evil of apartheid and identifying its villains in 2004 is easy. It is a far cry from taking a stand against it in 1984.

During last month's public drama of Nieuwoudt's amnesty hearing, we were reminded again of the choices that people can or cannot make when they are confronting their role in the evil of the past. De Kock seems to have crossed the threshold of guilt. He has done what most of his comrades have been unwilling or unable to do and admitted that apartheid's war, what he fought all his life, was wrong and a waste. He expressed a public apology to the families of the victims of the crime that is the subject of Nieuwoudt's amnesty hearing, and evoked a deeply moving emotional response. This may only be symbolic, but this is where hope begins. This is the kind of public dialogue we need to move our country forward onto the road of healing and reconciliation.

Nieuwoudt, in contrast, has become tangled in a web of memory loss. Not only that, he has experts claiming that he is suffering from post-traumatic stress disorder (PTSD). It is as if he is saying, as the psychologically damaged victim of the past, that he cannot be expected to account for it. The diagnosis of PTSD in cases of perpetrators who came before the TRC has become something of a growth industry, and Nieuwoudt's claims of PTSD send a wrong message. The essential feature of PTSD is a life-threatening experience, or one that threatens one's physical integrity. The fundamental element of the experience is that it overwhelms the senses, and evokes a response with the following main components: intense fear, helplessness and horror. For PTSD to be diagnosed, there must be a clearly identifiable life-threatening experience, commensurate with the response of fear, powerlessness and helplessness. I have not seen Nieuwoudt's psychiatrist's report, but based on what I know about Nieuwoudt's role in the security forces, being in full control and inflicting harm and risking little or no danger to himself, I doubt that he could claim that he endured these cardinal features of PTSD.

We have to ask: did Nieuwoudt suffer a life-threatening experience? Or is the truth too threatening to his Christian self, to his perception of himself as morally human? What the court may have to deal with in Nieuwoudt's trial is a denial of memory rather than its loss. If he does show aberrant symptoms, the question has to be asked: are they symptoms of PTSD, or anxiety about the public shame and humiliation he has to endure? Are the truths he is forced to face about himself too threatening for him, so that he has to protect himself against internal rupture of his perception of himself as a moral human being, and undoing what he believed in for his entire life too frightening to confront?

The public behaviour of Nieuwoudt and De Kock represent two options in terms of how we may confront the past in our society. Let us make the choice that will uphold the vision of reconciliation and social change in our country.

7. The power of forgiveness

MAIL & GUARDIAN, 23 MARCH 2005

In February 2005, I was one of five South Africans, including Archbishop Desmond Tutu, who were invited to address an international symposium on Restorative Justice and Peace in Colombia. Attended by more than 1 000 people, it was meant to be a threshold moment in the history of Colombia, which had experienced nearly 50 years of conflict.

CALI, THE THIRD-LARGEST city in Colombia, is set in a beautiful green valley, amid mountains that stretch as far as the eye can see. From a distance, it looks like a tropical paradise, with palm trees stretching into the sky, warm weather, and a refreshingly cool evening breeze. But beauty is not the reason why we are in Colombia. We are the first to arrive of a group of South Africans invited to speak at a conference on restorative justice and peace.

It is late evening. Archbishop Desmond Tutu, his assistant Dan Vaughn and I are being driven to our hotel, an hour's drive from the airport. As we near the hotel, evidence of the tragic devastation suffered by ordinary Colombians unfolds before our eyes: shanty quarters flank the road, many of them built on top of each other, stretching for miles and covering the bottoms of the beautiful hills, their lights dotting the area and cascading down into the valley in what would otherwise have been a 'prime location', against the backdrop of the elegant mountainside that is typical of the Colombian landscape.

Colombians are tired of the cycles of violence that have dominated their lives and plunged them into the doldrums of poverty and fear. They want peace, and freedom from fear. That is why we were in Cali last month, five South Africans invited to address the first international conference on restorative justice and peace in

Colombia: Albie Sachs, Tutu, Penuell Maduna, Tokyo Sexwale and I.[6] One could say we were in Colombia as ambassadors of South Africa's peaceful transition.

In my international travels and public lectures on forgiveness and dialogue, I have been amazed by how much South Africa continues to enjoy respect globally as the country that success-fully carved out a unique approach to democratic transition, and created a new language for dealing with past conflict, the language of reconciliation.

No one epitomised the role that South Africa has come to play in countries emerging from conflict more than Tutu. When he spoke about hope as only he can, hope as something we can all touch, the audience in the full-to-capacity conference hall rose to its feet, applauded, and shouted cheers of excitement. The hunger for peace was palpable. It reminded me of the excitement and hope generated at once by the South African negotiation process, the 1994 elections, and the Truth and Reconciliation Commission (TRC). 'We belong in a moral universe,' Tutu said in his opening address. 'There is no way in which evil can prevail.' And to a stand-ing ovation that reverberated throughout the huge hall and echoed far beyond, he concluded: 'Ultimately, goodness, joy, laughter and peace will prevail – these are God's gifts to you.'

All the South African speakers had one message for the Colombians: to tell the story of a country that was ravaged by years of violence, fear and anger, but sought dialogue instead of revenge. Sachs spoke about the importance of the South African constitution and 'the honour of being the generation that broke the cycles of violence and domination'. He related his own encounter with Henri, the apartheid security policeman who tried to kill

---

[6] At that time, Albie Sachs was a judge in the South African Constitutional Court, Tokyo Sexwale a businessman and former premier of Gauteng, and Penuell Maduna a former Minister of Justice.

him, Henri's quest to meet him to ask his forgiveness, and the first time he shook Henri's hand after he had testified before the TRC. Sachs movingly described the process of creating a constitution that captures the essence of transformation, and explained why the Old Fort in Braamfontein, Johannesburg, was chosen to house the Constitutional Court.

'The site of pain, the site of negativity, is the very site we chose to build a Constitutional Court that defends the rights of everyone. We took negative energy and turned it into something capable of creating beauty,' he said, referring to the role of the Old Fort as a prison from the late 19th century until 1987, and the cycles of hatred that the building had come to embody over the decades. That these cycles of hate were broken, Sachs said, was owed to the 'spirit of humanity, the sense of humanity that can be found anywhere in the world'.

The spirit of humanity was indeed present among Colombians themselves. Every Colombian we met could tell of family members who had been kidnapped or killed during a kidnapping, or the children of friends or neighbours who had been forced to join one of the parties involved in the Colombian war. There seemed to be some urgency among family members of victims of kidnappings to tell their stories; they wanted to speak to anyone who would hear their tales. Patricia, a young mother of two teenage sons, was among them.

If the wounded can be healers who can bring peace in a land torn by violence, Patricia, whose husband was kidnapped by members of the Revolutionary Armed Forces of Colombia, or FARC, would be one. She was one of many voices calling for peace in Colombia: 'I do not want these people who kidnapped my husband to go to jail,' Patricia said through the simultaneous translation. 'That will only lead to more violence; their children will revolt. All I want is for my husband to return to us, alive. If peace negotiations are not implemented, if this decades-old problem in Colombia is not resolved, I fear my children might become vengeful. I pray that this does not happen.'

Patricia had highlighted a well-known psychological consequence of trauma: how mutable the roles of victim and perpetrator are, and how easily cycles of violence are repeated and passed on intergenerationally, transforming victims into the embodiment of what they hate in the other.

At the end of a workshop I held at the conference on trauma and forgiveness, two women came up from behind and tapped me on my shoulder. One of the participants in the workshop immediately volunteered to act as translator between their Spanish and my English. The first woman wanted to talk about her husband who had been kidnapped three years previously. It was hard for her to mention his name; she hadn't done so for a long time. The last time she had heard from her husband's capturers was shortly after he was kidnapped. 'Having your husband captured is the most unbearable thing that could happen to anyone. But there is nothing worse than not hearing from those who are keeping him captive,' she said, her voice breaking.

The second woman's two young sons had been kidnapped. She tried to describe how she had heard about the kidnapping of the younger, who was 10 at the time, but the more she tried, the harder it was for her to tell his story. She began to choke up, and as she tried to continue, she broke down in uncontrollable sobs.

Silence about one's pain, I thought to myself, is a heavy burden that no one should carry. Earlier at the conference, Sexwale introduced Mpho Hani, who had been widowed when Chris Hani was assassinated by the white right-wingers Janusz Walus and Clive Derby-Lewis. (During his amnesty hearing at the TRC, Derby-

Lewis said he couldn't apologise for an 'act of war'.) Mpho's quiet tears as she was introduced were testimony to how silence freezes the pain of trauma and its associated emotions. However, she is also an example of the immeasurable capacity for human goodness even after so much trauma. Talking to her during a lunch break at the conference, I was struck by her commitment to the reconciliation agenda in South Africa.

At the centre of the strife in Colombia are various groups: left-wing organisations that were originally established as a liberation force against conservative rule in Colombia; the National Liberation Army, or ELN; the Revolutionary Armed Forces of Colombia; drug cartels; and paramilitary 'self-defence' units which were originally created to help the government fight left-wing organisations, but were subsequently outlawed.

On the last day of the conference, the Colombian president, Alvaro Uribe Velez, appeared in a televised dialogue with Tutu, Maduna and Sexwale. Sexwale delivered a pointed message to the guerrilla groups. 'Those of us who have fought for the freedom of our people,' he said, 'not once ever thought of kidnapping as a strategy for liberation. ... We compromise not because we fear war, but because we love peace more.'

The audience roared with applause, and rose to a lengthy ovation. 'No fighter worth any respect as a fighter will kidnap other people,' Sexwale declared. Addressing to Velez, he continued: 'Mr President, it is time for courage... As a citizen of the world, I say, rise from being a president – presidents come and go – to being a statesman.'

Maduna spoke about how he had once been called a 'cockroach' by a prison warder when he was a liberation fighter. He asked Velez whether he had ever reflected on the real needs of those fighting the state, and how he was planning to include them in the political negotiations that were being discussed in Colombia. 'Out there on the mountains are fellow human beings,' Maduna said. 'We must draw them out and bring them down into the valleys, if any process of negotiation is going to succeed.'

Colombia is one of the most troubled countries in the world. As always, those affected by the strife there are the most vulnerable members of society: woman, children, peasant farmers and ethnic minorities. The long and painful list of countries currently facing immeasurable strife and genocide shows that the world's most vulnerable are displaced and voiceless. They are hungry for peace, and long for normalcy in their lives. Countries such as Colombia, and many others on our own continent, highlight what was the moral challenge of the past century, and will be the central moral challenge of this century: as member countries of the United Nations, what should our response be to the destruction of the voiceless?

Well, Tutu, Maduna and Sexwale showed in Colombia how 'citizens of the world' can become alternative voices to lead international responses to countries whose citizens are crying out for peace. In response to Velez's not-so-overt plea for help from the South Africans, the South African threesome issued a joint statement, read by Tutu, making a commitment to approach President Thabo Mbeki in order to facilitate initial talks aimed at encouraging warring factions to join in dialogue with the Colombian government. 'Come down from the mountain,' Tutu called out to the fighters through the live TV broadcast; 'come down to help rebuild your country, Colombia.'

It may be a small gesture from South Africans, but when the people of Colombia responded with a standing ovation, it was as if Tutu's statement was enough to move mountains.

8. The language of forgiveness

Sunday Times, 17 July 2005

In June 2005, I had the honour of delivering a speech alongside a child survivor of the Holocaust at an event entitled '60 Years Later – Children of War Remember', hosted by the Kulturwissenschaftliches Institut in Germany. It brought together both victims of the Holocaust and family members of Nazi perpetrators. The depth and openness of mutual engagement illuminated for me the path that South Africa as a nation has yet to walk.

LAST MONTH I was invited to deliver a speech entitled 'Forgiveness as an issue of collective memory' at a public event organised by the Kulturwissenschaftliches Institut in Essen, Germany. The second lecture was entitled 'Auschwitz, Mengele, me and forgiveness', and its author, Eva Mozes Kor, was a child survivor of Dr Josef Mengele's so-called 'twin experiments' in the Nazi concentration camp of Auschwitz.

Some may wonder if the language of forgiveness is appropriate in discussions of historical memory in Germany, perhaps because of the word's erroneous association with forgetting. Far from being driven by a desire to forget, the men and women I met during my recent trip to Germany were fully confronting the past. They are the generation whose parents and relatives were the 'willing executioners' – as Daniel Goldhagen refers to Nazi-era German society – in Hitler's 'Final Solution'.

At the end of the war, the war generation was in denial, and wanted to forget the past and their role therein. When the post-war generation came of age in the 1960s and 1970s, however, they rebelled against their parents' denial of responsibility for the Holocaust. They self-righteously attacked their parents' generation for bringing Hitler to power. At the same time, they continued to enjoy the many privileges of an economically prosperous Germany.

Now in their mature years, having raised their own children, with most of the war generation beyond the grave, many Germans over the age of 50 are beginning to confront memories that they have shared only privately. The post-war generation in Germany is faced with the problem of guilt by association, and wants to deal with it not with the denial and veil of silence that followed the war. They want to confront their shame and guilt, embrace it, and transcend it. Dialogue about forgiveness and/or reconciliation may be the vehicle to reach that transcendence.

Unlike Germans, we South Africans had an opportunity, through the Truth and Reconciliation Commission (TRC) process, for public dialogue about our own past that created victims and perpetrators, beneficiaries and bystanders. In spite of the TRC process of public dialogue, however, and hardly a decade since the TRC concluded its work, we seem to be avoiding any reference to South Africa's horrific past and its wide-ranging consequences. We have become skilled at attacking one another – black and white – in private and in public. Whites accuse blacks of benefiting from post-apartheid privilege; blacks accuse whites of attitudes that serve to perpetuate the racism of the past. What is starkly missing is dialogue that could help us to understand the forces of the past.

South Africans can learn from the introspection of the generation of Germans who are courageously facing their country's history 60 years after Nazi atrocities in which they did not participate, and which they did not witness. The past, as the German writer Christa Wolf informs us, is not dead; it has not even passed.

We must talk about our difficult past, and how it continues to define our relationships in subtle ways. Through the dialogue about our past, we must also find a way of celebrating humanity. The heart of forgiveness does not necessarily lie in loving those around us (it definitely does not lie in hating them either). The spirit of forgiveness lies in the search – not for the things that separate us – but for something common among us as fellow human beings, the compassion and empathy that binds our human identity.

9. A wounded nation

Mail & Guardian, 23 December 2009

> *Listening to the comments of parishioners of St George's Cathedral in
> Cape Town on a Reconciliation Day pilgrimage, I was struck by how
> seldom South Africans have an opportunity to express their frustra-
> tions with our adolescent democracy. I wrote this reflection 15 years
> after the birth of our democracy, yet the need for continued dialogue
> is even more pronounced today.*

ON 16 DECEMBER 2009, Reconciliation Day, while many
Capetonians were driving towards the beaches, the dean of St
George's Cathedral, Rowan Smith, was welcoming a group of
people who had gathered for a two-hour pilgrimage. As a site of
resistance against apartheid, St George's Cathedral has long been
an important symbol of peace and unity. Here, religious leaders
of different faith groups joined hands with tens of thousands of
South Africans during apartheid to campaign for peace. Thus the
pilgrimage included stops at the Great Synagogue near the Cape
Town Gardens and the Palm Tree Mosque in Long Street.

The fact that the crowd of people who joined the pilgrimage did
not match the massive numbers witnessed at the Cathedral's peace
marches during the apartheid years suggests that the pilgrimage
does not carry as much urgency as campaigns in the past. Yet,
listening to the conversations, and watching the determination
on the faces of the racially diverse crowd walking towards the
Great Synagogue along the tree-lined Government Avenue in the
Company Gardens, one was reminded of the hunger for dialogue
among many South Africans from different racial groups.

'We need more of these kinds of events that bring us together,'
says a middle-aged white woman as she tries to catch up with me.

Her companion, a younger woman, agrees. She attended a public dialogue about reconciliation at the University of Cape Town the previous week, which addressed the challenges South Africans face in a post-apartheid society. 'There is so much anger and negative stuff we hear and read about,' she says, 'but there is also a lot of hope. This is why I try to attend these events – to keep alive the hope I have for my country.' As we leave the Great Synagogue and head towards the Palm Tree Mosque, two women, French and Italian, join me. They lament the small number of black people participating in the pilgrimage, especially those 'from the townships'. These observations, of anger and 'negative stuff', and of the apparent absence of black people 'from the townships' in reconciliation events, capture the story of South Africa 15 years after our democracy.

While there are a multitude of ways in which one could attempt to characterise the 'national psyche' of South Africans in the first decade of our democracy, I would like to offer two central, related themes. On the one hand, there is a great deal of anger and frustration among black and white South Africans for reasons that are different for each group. On the other, the spirit of reconciliation and sense of hope that reverberated throughout the country during the years of the Truth and Reconciliation Commission (TRC), which inspired a transformed conception of politics and society, have dissipated.

Behind the anger and frustration are enduringly painful emotional experiences that could be described as collective trauma. Many white South Africans, especially those whose votes sustained the apartheid government's oppressive rule, find it difficult to acknowledge that the social, educational and economic privileges under apartheid gave them a better life, and also created the possibility of a better future for them in the post-apartheid era.

Part of the collective denial of this status of beneficiaries has to do with the following: acknowledging that they have benefited from a system that oppressed fellow human beings, and even committed atrocities, threatens white people's sense of humanity. They need the psychological protection that denial provides to shield them from guilt and from recognising the justifications they need to avoid confronting the fact of the injustice of apartheid. Thus many will say: 'It is because of hard work and not privileges handed down to us by an oppressive system.' What is missing from this assertion is that black people worked hard. Their hard work, however, was not rewarded, and did not open doors in the same way as it did for whites, for example, in the ability to invest in property. Another complicating factor is that although apartheid was understood as a system that oppressed blacks (in all their diversity), the details of the repressive system of the apartheid state were not always in plain sight. Moreover, even if they were, fear and being in a comfort zone made it difficult for many whites to question apartheid, and actually take a stand against it.

There are other reasons for the collective denial by many white South Africans that they benefited from apartheid. The racial superiority and life of privilege bestowed on many white people a kind of certainty about their future and the future of their children. There was a time when white families knew which university their children would attend, what programmes they would register for, and what company they would join afterwards. These certainties have been shattered, and for some whites the loss of these privileges has led to real emotional pain. At a group level, these emotions may be experienced as a kind of collective trauma, and may lead to feelings of victimhood.

What I am saying is that most of the anger we have witnessed among whites stems from a real sense of loss – a loss of privilege, and a feeling of powerlessness in a society that seems to privilege blacks. For the majority of black people, however, the scales of privilege are tilted towards the very few: the beneficiaries of black economic empowerment, and those with ministerial power to allocate material privileges to themselves.

So, while President Jacob Zuma says we have a constitution that guarantees human rights for all, the experience on the ground is that very little has changed, or is changing. Some schools for black learners around the country are in an appalling physical state. Some learners who pass matric from these schools have never seen a microscope, yet, when they enrol at a university, they are expected to compete with their peers as if they have had the same educational experience.

In their 1989 book *Uprooting Poverty – The South African Challenge,*[7] Francis Wilson and Mamphela Ramphele characterised the deep economic divisions in our society as the distinction between 'grinding poverty and massive wealth'. Twenty years later, this situation still prevails, and some may say it has become worse. The difference is that some of the massive wealth is now in the hands of a minority of blacks who are beneficiaries of the privileges of black economic empowerment.

While we have witnessed mutual distrust and racial hostility among some black and white South Africans, such feelings among black people may reflect frustration arising from a lack of opportunities available to break the cycles of poverty. Many young black people wake up to a yawning void of emptiness, with no opportunities for skills training, jobs or inspiration to attend the schools in their neighbourhoods. They are caught up in a never-ending cycle of nothingness. We should not be surprised that, increasingly, we

---

[7]   Francis Wilson and Mamphela Ramphele, *Uprooting Poverty – The South African Challenge*, Cape Town: David Philip, 1989.

see more young people taking to the streets in protest, and that the age of the perpetrators of violent crime is becoming younger.

The 15 years of our democracy seem to have produced a generation of young people whose circumstances make them feel worthless. This makes it difficult to bestow worth upon others, and to connect with them as fellow human beings. This is how poverty strips away the humanity of individuals.

The complex and enduring struggle to restore one's sense of humanity in the face of such dehumanising conditions can manifest in violence, against self or others. Gatherings such as the St George's Cathedral pilgrimage remind us of the importance of walking the journeys that bring us back to the table of shared humanity. This solidarity is perhaps what we need to face our psychological demons, and to repair the brokenness of our society across racial and generational divides. The words of the psychoanalyst Robert Stolorow capture this sentiment: 'If we can help one another bear the darkness rather than evade it, perhaps one day we will be able to see the light.'

We need a new vision of humanism. We need to find ways to listen to one another's stories of pain. This will enable us to extend our ethical horizons to include others, and to understand that we are implicated in one another's pain and trauma.

10. Towards an anatomy of violence

MAIL & GUARDIAN, 15 JANUARY 2010

In October 1996, Eugene de Kock was sentenced to 212 years in prison for crimes committed while serving as commander of the apartheid-era counter-insurgency police unit stationed at Vlakplaas, west of Pretoria.[8] When, in January 2010, newspapers announced that De Kock was seeking a presidential pardon from Jacob Zuma, this led to a public outcry.[9] In this article, I sought to place the reactions in a psychological perspective, and to explain why I believed his request should be granted.

SOME NAMES HAVE become synonymous with torture, murder, and other crimes against humanity in the 20th and 21st centuries. The Belgian King Leopold II and the colonial genocide in the Congo; Adolf Hitler and the Holocaust in Nazi Germany; Pol Pot and the Cambodian 'killing fields'; Slobodan Milošević and his campaign of 'ethnic cleansing' in Kosovo; Charles Taylor and the massacres of Sierra Leone, all conjure up images of the most unimaginable state-orchestrated crimes. These were men of power, architects of destructive regimes which they led and sustained with the help of their lieutenants.

---

[8]   De Kock was convicted on six counts of murder as well charges of conspiracy to commit murder, attempted murder, culpable homicide, being an accessory to culpable homicide, defeating the ends of justice, assault, kidnapping, fraud, and the illegal possession of weapons and explosives. He was convicted to two life sentences as well as 212 years' imprisonment, but the sentences were to run concurrently. See Sapa, 'Two life sentences, 212 years' imprisonment for De Kock', 30 October 1996, http://www.justice.gov.za/trc/media%5C1996%5C9610/s961030l.htm.

[9]   *The Week UK*, 'Eugene de Kock "looking for a presidential pardon"', 16 January 2010, http://www.theweek.co.uk/politics/17533/eugene-de-kock-%E2%80%98looking-presidential-pardon%E2%80%99; *Daily Maverick*, 'Just don't do it, Mr President', 4 January 2010, http://www.dailymaverick.co.za/article/2010-01-04-just-dont-do-it-mr-president/#.UxlhC4Wj0ns

Eugene de Kock was a 'lieutenant' of the apartheid regime. His name has become nearly synonymous with the regime's massive scale of state repression – the years of terror against those who were fighting for freedom ('enemies of the state'), and the extraordinary brutality of its covert counter-insurgency operations. For nearly 15 years, De Kock has been serving multiple sentences in C Max, the maximum security prison in Pretoria, for crimes he committed as the head of the apartheid government's security apparatus for covert operations at Vlakplaas, where he earned the nickname 'Prime Evil' from his colleagues. The label has stuck, and with it the perception of De Kock in our collective consciousness as the embodiment of all that is evil about our country's past.

De Kock's name has re-entered the public arena with rumours of his possible release by presidential pardon, evoking predictable images of 'the evil one' ingrained in our collective memory, and of the deeds committed by the man who has to carry the burden of uncomfortable truths about our past. I interviewed De Kock for several hours over three months in 1997 following his first appearance at a public hearing of the Truth and Reconciliation Commission (TRC), when family members of victims killed during Vlakplaas operations met with him for the first time. The main inspiration for the interviews was a desire to integrate several themes I was interested in at the time, themes that continue to exercise my mind.

To my knowledge, the expressions of apology, remorse and forgiveness witnessed at the TRC (though very few) were unprecedented in the history of atrocities. Until the TRC, experts had argued that the language of apology, forgiveness and reconciliation was beyond the purview of acts of the kind reported at the TRC's public hearings. However, they were proved wrong. I was interested in understanding the significance – for individual

victims, and for our post-apartheid society – of public acknowledgement of, and accountability for, past violations and suffering,
what the phenomena of remorse and forgiveness mean, and how
they emerge in encounters between family members who have lost
irreparably on the one hand, and perpetrators responsible for the
loss on the other.

One other factor shaped my interest in these themes. Before
joining the TRC, I had spent many hours interviewing perpetrators
of 'necklace' murders in Mlungisi township in Queenstown for my
doctoral thesis. The hours I spent with the young men and women
who had been involved in 'necklace' murders, and with members
of the Mlungisi community who had witnessed those gruesome
murders, convinced me that the label 'evil' fails to capture the
complexity of social and political dynamics at play when ordinary people are induced to commit, or tacitly support, murderous
violence. Simply to label as 'evil' actions that dehumanise, torture
or kill other human beings in the context of collective violence
and state-orchestrated abuse tends to stifle efforts to understand
the roots of past hatred and violence, and may silence debate on
the continuing legacy of the past in the present. Thus the desire to
understand the anatomy of violence, and how ordinary people are
transformed into perpetrators of horrific acts, was the impetus for
my interviews with De Kock.

A question that most people have asked concerning De Kock
is whether he deserves to be released. Those who oppose the idea
of his release argue that he is too tainted with the blood of victims,
too 'evil' to be allowed to rejoin the world of moral humanity. Yet,
how 'innocent', how 'pure' is our society of free men and women? It
is not very long ago that we witnessed our young white men being
sent to fight the apartheid government's war against freedom fighters across our borders. De Kock was introduced to the badge of

'evil' he has to wear through the same system of army conscription at the tender age of 16.

Where are these men who fought the same battles as De Kock in Rhodesia, Namibia and Mozambique, what did they do in the service of apartheid, and what painful and gruesome secrets do they harbour? Have we forgotten the times when we faced the cruel irony of watching or reading about black vigilante groups and young white soldiers killing black people in the townships in the name of rooting out communism? My point is not to drag us to the past, but rather to confront the reality that there are many South Africans who are implicated – directly or indirectly – in the deeds that De Kock committed. Very few people raised their voices to stop the state-orchestrated violence against the oppressed and disenfranchised people of South Africa.

'Even when pressed by the demands of inner truth,' the slain American civil rights leader Martin Luther King reminds us, 'men do not easily assume the task of opposing their government's policy, especially in time of war.' Additionally, collective violence and violence committed by armies and state security police are not the result of the actions of sadists and deranged psychopaths – far from it. There is no doubt that in times of political conflict, some perpetrators may be psychopaths. Let us consider, however, that numerous social psychology studies have shown that most ordinary human beings can be initiated into evil by persuasive messages, for example messages of 'die swart gevaar' (the black threat), or by compelling force of circumstances which lead them to believe that they are involved in a moral course. South Africa decided to approach the road to transformation by attempting to understand the causes of so much violence and hatred in our country, and by inviting perpetrators and bystanders to acknowledge the pain suffered by victims of all racial groups. Without much exaggeration, De Kock's role at the TRC was crucial, and at times pivotal, in terms of identifying some key actors in the brutality of the past.

My comments here are in no way a campaign to diminish De Kock's crimes, or to undermine the legacy of the traumatic loss caused by his actions. I believe, however, that keeping De Kock behind bars would encourage 'the great forgetting' – to paraphrase Adam Rothschild's description of the forgotten horrors of colonial Europe. Releasing him would open up the possibility of a movement towards a new politics of remembrance, one that would help invigorate dialogue about the kind of future we want, and the future of young South Africans. De Kock would remind us how easy it is to cultivate hatred, and that the repetition of destructive messages from people in positions of power can no longer be entertained as just metaphors.

Any act of pardon should take seriously the issue of whether perpetrators of gross human rights abuses have faced their past and reflected on the moral implications of their actions. The challenge, I think, is how to define morally reasonable grounds on which to grant perpetrators mercy, and allow them to re-enter society. These should include evidence of remorseful regret, and a commitment to efforts aimed at ensuring that South Africans never fight one another again in a war.

People who fail to see the senselessness of the bloodshed of the apartheid regime, who have not faced their guilt and learned to grieve for the violent loss of so many innocent lives, should be watched closely. Conservative Party member Clive Derby Lewis, for example, who with Polish right-winger Janusz Walus, is serving a life term for the murder of the South African Communist Party leader Chris Hani, made his attitude clear before the TRC: 'How can I apologise for an act of war? War is war.'

Mercy? Mercy should be granted cautiously. Our society should consider embracing those who, like De Kock, could make an important contribution to the historical consciousness of South Africa's past, and ensure that the history of what happened to victims is not repressed. Facing the past – acknowledgement of past wrongs by perpetrators, bystanders and beneficiaries alike – is the touchstone of reconciliation. Reconciliation has become a dirty word, and some people see it as a masquerade for impunity. The value of reconciliation politics, however, is that it shifts from an exclusive focus on prosecutions to allow the emergence of a profoundly new politics of engagement with the past, not in order to rekindle old hatreds, but rather to learn from them.

Samantha Power, winner of the Pulitzer Prize for her book *A Problem from Hell*, suggests that the adage 'never again!' should be changed to 'again and again'. I think that 'never again' has a chance of becoming a reality in our country if we face the fact that 'Prime Evil' is not only on De Kock's face, but has the potential to be written on yours and mine as well. Eugene De Kock's name may be synonymous with the past horrors of the apartheid regime; however, the men of real power – the architects of apartheid destruction – continue to live in our midst, and some have died living among us. Moreover, most of them preferred the lie that there was nothing wrong with the system of apartheid to facing the immeasurable destruction that apartheid has caused in the lives of countless South Africans, black and white.

11. Rwanda draws strength from its pain

Mail & Guardian, 29 April 2011

In April 2011, I attended a week of events in Rwanda commemorating the 17th anniversary of the genocide in that country. An encounter with a young Rwandan filmmaker impressed upon me the need to face shameful memories of the past with courage, and I wanted to share his story with the many South Africans who bear haunting memories of the suffering of others.

IT IS THE end of a week of commemorative events throughout Rwanda to mark the 17th anniversary of the genocide of the Tutsi people, which took place between April and July 1994. I am in Kigali, the capital of Rwanda, and the 27-year-old poet and filmmaker Edouard Bamporiki is sharing his painful memories – those of a child who witnessed the carnage.

The first time that Bamporiki realised he was a Hutu was when he was eight years old. He was in grade three, and his teacher gave the class 'homework' – to ask their parents what their ethnic groups were. The following day, after the pupils had revealed their ethnic identity to the teacher, Bamporiki was excited to learn that his ethnicity was in the majority. The feeling of excitement he describes is one of child-like innocence, a feeling of the strength of his identity in numbers. 'We immediately formed ourselves into Hutu and Tutsi soccer teams,' he says. Because his Tutsi classmates did not have enough on their side to form a team, 'we gave them some Hutus, and we started playing against each other'.

A year later, Bamporiki was to witness how that playful response to the issue of difference could be transformed on a national stage into genocide. At the end of it, and when the schools reopened, none of the Tutsi boys he had played soccer with returned. 'I was so confused,' he says. 'They were my friends.' Bamporiki witnessed at first hand the horrors that became commonplace in every town and village. He wrote his first poem, whose title in his home language translates into the words, 'If they were not exterminated, we would be laughing together'. He continued to write poems about the genocide ('I write because of this cross,' he says), and won awards and invitations to recite his poetry at genocide commemoration events.

The recent commemorations that took place across Rwanda recalled the genocide in which an estimated one million Tutsis and some Hutus were slaughtered, a bloody rampage that went on for 100 days. The start of the commemorative period – seven days of mourning beginning on 7 April – was marked by a solemn event in a packed and overflowing 40 000-seater stadium in Kigali. At times, the quiet and stillness in that stadium were overwhelming. Then, during solemn speeches, there were outbursts of wailing and the sound of sobbing – but even the people's grief had a sense of quiet reverence.

The Rwandan president, Paul Kagame, captured that sense when he spoke in his native Kinyarwanda language to the thousands of survivors and mourners packed in and around the stadium. One could sense, even without using the simultaneous translation service, the urgency in Kagame's voice. Speaking under a banner proclaiming the theme 'Upholding Truth: Preserving Our Dignity', Kagame said: 'The body of Rwanda was tortured, assaulted and succumbed, but the spirit never died.' He chose his words carefully to convey his meaning clearly to each of the thousands of Rwandans who had come to mourn their dead collectively, as a nation, for the 17th time. 'There is a lot of pain and sadness,' he said, 'but we have to take seriously the meaning of these two words: truth and dignity.'

An earlier public testimony by a survivor of the genocide gave weight to the notion of dignity; violation destroyed the human spirit, and stripped victims of their dignity. To bear witness to the stories of family members of victims and the survivors of such horrific crimes in essence honours their memory, acknowledges their humanity, and helps them to reclaim their sense of dignity. These testimonies also have a significance that sometimes goes beyond the lives of victims and survivors to move others to speak truthfully in ways that they were previously unable, or afraid, to do.

Bamporiki gave a testimony of what he witnessed as a child when the genocide broke out on that day in April 1994. He had been admitted to hospital when the genocide broke out, and a man carrying a baby had hidden under his bed. Early the following morning, a group of machete-wielding men burst into the ward looking for Pierre [not his real name]. They were singing the 'genocide song', a song about killing all Tutsis, and were calling Pierre, telling him to come out.

When Bamporiki described the moment when Pierre spoke out from under the bed and said, 'I am here', the pain in his eyes was unmistakable. 'I can never, ever forget that voice that pierced through me from under my bed at the hospital,' he said. What he saw next, and Pierre's piercing voice, is a scene that remains etched in his memory no matter how hard he tries to forget. Pierre laid dead on the floor, the baby still in his arms. Then one of the men killed the baby in Pierre's dead arms.

I visited the Kigali Genocide Memorial. It contains the remains of 250 000 people buried in mass graves covered in wide slabs of concrete, slabs that cascade down several levels of the garden sanctuary. Some of the graves are framed in borders of face brick that make them look like flower beds, and roses are planted on top of the graves. The roses, unlike those carefully manicured flowers in the many gardens around Kigali (landscaping is very much a feature of the city), are carefully stripped of their leaves so that they look like desolate flowers growing in the desert, yielding beauty in spite of what lies beneath. As we drove south from Kigali to Butare, the driver pointed out several marked mass graves. Butare is the site of the Murambi Memorial, which houses the most visible aspects of the genocide against the Tutsi.

The Rwandan countryside is one of the most beautiful landscapes I have ever seen – the hills roll into each other with stunning green beauty. It is simply unbelievable that, scattered in the hills and forests of this beautiful country (Rwandans call it the country of a thousand hills), are mass graves as yet undiscovered. But Rwanda is healing itself. The Rwandans' journey after the genocide is an incredible story of a search for lasting peace, unity and economic stability.

To have witnessed such a dearth of humanity reminded me of the history of my own country. There are similarities, yet the differences are also quite significant. One difference is that Rwanda is facing its past, confronting it, but is careful to emphasise learning from the past to prevent its repetition. 'When we say never again, it means exactly that – we should never allow this to happen again,' Kagame said in his speech at the stadium in Kigali. 'Fellow Rwandans, the sadness and pain we have is understandable, but we should draw strength from this to heal ourselves and to build our future.'

He was echoing the sentiment in the famous words of Spanish philosopher George Santayana, who remarked that 'those who do not remember the past are condemned to repeat it'. Facing our history and confronting our shame about it can help us understand how human depravity creeps in ever so imperceptibly. Dialogue about a past characterised by racial mistrust and different dimensions of violence could help restore confidence and trust in our future. Facing each other in the spirit of dialogue could also help us reclaim the better angels of our nature.

Bamporiki said that for many years he was burdened by shame as a Hutu. Once, when he travelled to France to receive an award for one of his films, he was asked by a Frenchman if he had killed any Tutsis. 'Come on now, Edouard,' the Frenchman said, 'you are Hutu, you must have killed some Tutsis.' Bamporiki could not respond.

Flying back home, he realized that his shame for having witnessed the slaughter of Tutsis and having the 'advantage' of being Hutu was a noose. Engaging that past, both directly and in creative ways, has helped him heal the shame. His award-winning film *Long Coat* is about a Hutu man who refuses to confess to killing his neighbour. But it is also more than that. His screening of the film in a prison in Kigali prompted the inmates who had participated in the genocide to organise the first-ever confessional commemoration of the genocide by the prisoners themselves.

From the stories of Tutsi and Hutu students at the national University of Rwanda forming reconciliation clubs, of the 'genocide widows' in Karama village in the south working with women whose husbands are serving prison terms for the genocide, and of the orphans joining forces to create 'families' to support one another at university, there is real hope and a prospect for peace in Rwanda. And, judging from the way Rwandans speak about Kagame and the morale they say he inspires, and in spite of his faults, he seems to carry the hope of his people on his shoulders and in his heart.

12. What we must remember

Sunday Times, 25 March 2012

Bloemfontein, former capital of the Republic of the Orange Free State, houses divergent commemorations of the traumatic confrontation between the British Empire and the Boer republics at the turn of the 19th century. Troubled by plaques in a cathedral praising British heroism in a war that produced the world's first concentration camps, I reflected on the persistence of unresolved conflicts, and a more recent commemoration in a small Free State town that contains the seeds of the restoration of our human solidarity.

THE ANGLICAN CATHEDRAL in Bloemfontein is a magnificent building. As I drive into the church grounds, the cathedral with its impressive size in front of me, I am amazed at how beautiful the sprawling grounds are, with rows of trees at first glance looking like a beautiful mini forest, an imaginary stream in my mind's eye running through it.

Walking through this elegantly manicured garden/miniature forest to join the Sunday service inside, I feel as if I am surrounded by spiritual splendour, soft sounds of angels hovering gracefully above in joyful praise. Inside the cathedral, my eyes travel through the expanse of its interior and are drawn to the exquisite stained-glass windows far in the front, behind the altar and high above it, just below the ceiling on both sides of the church. Later, I notice the same awe-inspiring Victorian grandeur at the back of the cathedral, complementing the windows at the front end of the church with graceful elegance.

Being in the presence of such aesthetic beauty, with the glorious sounds of the organ in the background, it is difficult to imagine the people who sat in these pews and sang these same hymns to have been anything other than good people, loving their neighbours in the tradition of their faith. Yet this place of worship – whose first stone was laid by a British army major, Henry Warden, a deed that earned him recognition for giving Bloemfontein its 'spiritual heart' – was probably as exquisite and peaceful when women and children were forced into concentration camps erected by the British at the dawn of the 20th century as it was last Sunday.

Walking around the cathedral after the service, I am astonished by the many plaques commemorating soldiers who served in the 'Orange River Colony'. One of those plaques celebrates the memory of Lord Frederick Roberts, whose right-hand man, Lord Kitchener, imposed the brutal 'scorched earth' policy of destruction on Boer farms and their homes. How can this be, I wonder – such brazen celebration of the history of an atrocity in the city that has one of the first national monuments in the world dedicated to women? The National Women's Monument, dedicated to the Boer women and children who died in British concentration camps, and the Anglo-Boer War Museum, which recounts experiences of Boer and black African people during the Anglo-Boer War, were the first places I visited when I came to Bloemfontein last month. With the memory of those visits still fresh in my mind, taking in the narrative of the heroism portrayed on the walls of the cathedral was challenging.

A dedication of the lights in the cathedral by 'Brother Officers' in 1903; a plaque 'in memory of the men of the South African Constabulary' in 1900; and a giving of thanks for the men who had lost their lives and served in the Orange River Colony in 1900 – those dedications and plaques in bronze and stone seemed to form a rhythm of enactment of the past on the walls of the church, with the silent voices of victims in the background an open reality.

As I exit the small chapel adjoining the main church, also built in memory of the 'soldiers who died in the Orange River Colony', my attention is drawn to a more contemporary commemorative stone, unveiled on 27 April 1994. The last sentence in the inscription on the stone reads, 'We give thanks for a new South Africa'. The 'new' South Africa was very visible in the racially mixed congregation and clergy in the cathedral's Sunday morning service.

Driving away from the cathedral, however, I felt a sense of disquiet. Like all commemorative images, memorial plaques are an appeal for solidarity with families of those whose lives are remembered. Yet, for me, the commemorative plaques in the cathedral seemed to make the double historical trauma of the war and the British concentration camps in which thousands died, more visible; the presence of the past was 'uncannily real', to paraphrase the German philosopher Jürgen Habermas.

Habermas, of course, was referring to the memory of another era of concentration camps – that of the Nazi concentration camps, 40 years after the liberation of Jews from these camps. Without any attempt to compare the evil of the British concentration camps in South Africa to the evil of the Nazi camps in Germany and Poland, I wonder why the atrocity on South African soil has not been addressed with equal force? Could the reason be that the survivors were able to recover, build a proud Afrikaner nation, and 'move on'? Survivors of the Holocaust also built a proud Jewish nation in Israel. Yet human solidarity with the Holocaust has continued to produce 'witnesses' across the globe ('secondary witnesses' as they have been called), resulting in a constant flow of intergenerational dialogue about the Holocaust that has humanised its victims and, some would argue, helped the world to draw moral lessons from it.

Neither the 'silence' of the historical trauma of the concentration camps in South Africa, nor the injunction to speak about the Holocaust in future generations, has had significant success in producing the kind of compelling moral lessons that inspire lasting peace and democratic values in societies with histories of mass violence. For instance, the suffering of civilians in South Africa's violent historical past at the beginning of the 20th century was followed later by the systematic dehumanisation of civilians under apartheid. The inability to face the moral issues of the past plays itself out in repetition and continues to haunt us in the silence of apartheid's lambs, the denial of history, and the incessant call from some quarters in our country to 'forget the past and move on'.

Some comfort, then, however tenuous, may come from the memory of one of South Africa's courageous voices, Beyers Naudé, whom Nelson Mandela once referred to as the 'living spring of hope for racial reconciliation'. It is a memory evoked in the reflective space of my driving away from the cathedral and remembering a hymn sung earlier, one composed by Charles Coffin, the rector of the University of Paris in the early 18th century, about love for one's neighbour.

In essence, love for one's neighbour is an appeal to human empathy. Naudé grasped the meaning of this call when he condemned the inhumanity of apartheid. When the Dutch Reformed Church rejected him, he explained to his congregation that he was following the tradition of his faith by placing 'the authority of God before the authority of man'. His words were part of his final sermon in his church, after which he is reported to have removed his priestly robe and left the building. He later established the non-racial Christian Institute, a vibrant body of theological scholarship with an anti-apartheid message.

In contemporary Bloemfontein, the rector of the University of the Free State, Jonathan Jansen, writing in his regular Monday Bulletin, tells the story of the inauguration of the university's dean of students into the ministry of the Dutch Reformed Church. He describes a moment during the inauguration, in the church of the small Free State town of Luckhoff, that strikes me as the kind of commemorative event that we need in these difficult times in our country because of the hope it inspires.

'Two women, one black and one white, the women who had raised [the dean of students],' writes Jansen, 'carried a heavy black cloak to lay across his shoulders. It was the [robe] once worn by that great South African preacher, reconciler and humanist Beyers Naudé.' This symbolic moment of the passing of the baton from a remarkable South African who lived his life with moral courage, who is the embodiment of human empathy, is what we need in our places of worship, more than commemorative plaques that celebrate past wars. It is a story that should be transmitted as a living memory across generations, in order to inspire the deep human solidarity that Naudé and others bestowed on our country during the worst of times, and to motivate our collective voices of witness about the aspects of our past that should not be repeated.

The robes of Archbishop Emeritus Desmond Tutu, Bishop David Russell, Imam Abdullah Haron, Reverend John Freeth – some of the contemporary South African clergy who engaged with apartheid with moral reflection – and of the German priest Dietrich Bonhoeffer, killed for standing up against Nazism in Germany, are symbols of the moral imagination that is possible in times of hateful violence. They should be passed on as part of public dialogue about the past. As a living memory that can inspire us to seek our better angels – the practice of human solidarity – these are the memories that can restore the bond of human solidarity in our streets.

13. Apologies aren't enough

THE BOSTON GLOBE, 20 SEPTEMBER 2013

In 1999, Dr Wen Ho Lee, a nuclear scientist working at the Los Alamos National Laboratory in New Mexico, was charged with mishandling classified government information. Following submissions by Federal authorities, Lee was denied bail and held in solitary confinement for 278 days. In September 2000, Judge James Parker of the US District Court in New Mexico apologised to Dr Lee for the 'unfair manner in which he had been held in custody by the Executive Branch'.[10]

THE APOLOGY BY Federal District Judge James Parker to the Los Alamos scientist Wen Ho Lee resonates with events in South Africa. However, it also addresses an issue that has so far been ignored in South Africa: bestowing on the one who suffered what was lost when the abuse was perpetrated.

South African history would have been written differently if only a few of the judges under apartheid had spoken out against the state's abuse of power, as Judge Parker has done in relation to the American government's role in the Wen Ho Lee case. The historical role of apartheid courts as enforcers of apartheid laws, and their failure to treat blacks equally to whites, is a memory that will not go away easily for black South Africans.

The courts did not stand at a critical distance from some of the oppressive and barbaric apartheid laws that brought misery to the majority of South Africa's citizens. For many blacks, the notion of 'protection under the law' had a hollow ring to it. When magistrates, judges, prosecutors, and investigating officers who served under apartheid were called by the Truth and Reconciliation

---

[10] For a full transcript of Parker's remarks, see www.wenholee.org/apology.

Commission to account for their actions, they declined, refusing to acknowledge their role, and failing to rise to the extraordinary historical moment to apologise at a time when such symbolic gestures played an important unifying role.

However, the South African judges' refusal to apologise is probably an insignificant loss in the larger scale of things. A more tragic loss cries out to be acknowledged. There was a tendency to identify the apologies uttered on the stage of the TRC with the process of transformation. This left the impression that the 'coming to terms' which occurred through the commission was somehow enough. It left the impression that all that was needed were statements of reconciliation issued by leaders, perpetrators, and victims alike. This is, of course, not the case.

Victims who told their stories of trauma to the commission still await the reparations they were promised: unemployment among young and old South Africans has become more visible than ever; black residential areas have become breeding grounds for criminals, particularly rapists who prey upon family and neighbours; many teacher training colleges have been closed down, and nothing much has been done to improve education for blacks; in the black township where I grew up, and where I visited in the summer, hardly a weekend went by without a funeral for someone with AIDS – and so on.

Those who are looking at the TRC as a model in conflicts – take note. A process of public accounting is important, because it forces people – not just those who dealt the murderous blows, but also those who failed to speak out against abuses of power – to come to terms with their capacity to do injustices. It reframes justice in a way that restores dignity and hope to those who suffered under an oppressive system. It is a chance for those who were responsible for the suffering to reclaim their humanity. However, the lesson of the TRC is that one shouldn't settle for utterances of apology and symbolic gestures of forgiveness and reconciliation. Instead, this transformative moment should be used to address strategies for real change.

The South African government has decided that the best way to do this is 'to build a black middle class'– as if a black middle class will behave any differently from whites during apartheid rule. The result is that only a small percentage of blacks are benefitting from such government policies as affirmative action, and no effective programmes are in place to improve the lot of the poor.

The danger of this is that if the greater challenge of economic transformation is not met, what has already been achieved in South Africa could be lost, and something worse could happen. The next revolution might not necessarily be a racial one, but one in which the masses rise against the new breed of beneficiaries of privilege.

DILEMMAS OF LEADERSHIP AND MORALITY

'It is a gruesome tale – how we have moved so rapidly from the era of hope to the bleak landscape ushered in by Zuma's ascent to power, how we find ourselves in a state characterised by poor service delivery, major corruption at all levels of government, increasing violence against women, and many other problems that have torn apart the moral fibre of our society.'

14. HIV/AIDS and the government's greatest crime

Mail & Guardian, 30 November 2001

The denial of the link between HIV and AIDS continues to affect South Africans long after Thabo Mbeki's presidency. I wrote this article after Mbeki's Inaugural ZK Matthews Memorial Lecture at the University of Fort Hare in October 2001 in which he perpetuated his AIDS denialism under the guise of Black Consciousness.[11]

PRESIDENT THABO MBEKI'S speech at Fort Hare will lay nothing to rest. His latest conspiracy theory about the AIDS issue – that AIDS statistics have more to do with derogatory views (that 'we' are 'promiscuous carriers of germs' with an 'unconquerable devotion to the sin of lust') than sexual behaviour – comes at a time when the nation may be approaching the darkest hour in the AIDS crisis.

South Africa, and the world beyond, has grown weary of the dangerous rhetoric of our leaders. A generation of young South Africans is looking up to a president who has freely and publicly expressed his views about the state of AIDS in the country. What are they learning? Mbeki's comments at Fort Hare have come hot on the heels of the controversy surrounding his blocking of the Medical Research Council's report on the impact of HIV/AIDS.[12]

---

[11] Thabo Mbeki, Inaugural ZK Matthews Memorial Lecture, University of Fort Hare, 12 October 2001, http://www.thepresidency.gov.za/pebble.asp?relid=2727.

[12] Rob Dorrington et al, *The Impact of HIV/AIDS on Adult Mortality in South Africa*, Technical Report, Burden of Disease Research Unit, Medical Research Council, September 2001, http://www.mrc.ac.za/bod/complete.pdf. The report found that AIDS had become the single biggest cause of death in South Africa, and warned that, without treatment to prevent AIDS, the number of AIDS deaths would grow to more than double the number of deaths due to all other causes, resulting in 5 to 7 million cumulative AIDS deaths by 2010.

What is disturbing about all this 'dithering' is that it has prevented real dialogue about the AIDS issue in our country. For instance, how can we have a public debate about the sexual behaviour of men who, with few exceptions, are notoriously promiscuous throughout most of Africa, if our president chooses to use political rhetoric to avoid confronting some of the most critical issues about the spread of AIDS in South Africa?

Great strides have been made by community organisations working on AIDS awareness programmes. The government has tried to lend its support in some areas. But one gets the feeling that there is an overwhelming sense of paralysis at the government level, and that politicians have simply decided to deny that there is a crisis.

Perhaps we shall hear no greater truth than the one revealed by Mbeki's spokesperson, Parks Mankahlana, just before he died. The straight-talking Parks cut through the government denials of the causal relationship between HIV and AIDS, repeated recently by the MEC for health in Mpumalanga, and said plainly: if we provide medication to save the babies of pregnant mothers with AIDS, the government will be faced with a new problem: the problem of orphans.

If the government can't save the country's unborn, it could at least save the living. Exactly six months since the pharmaceutical industry dropped a suit aimed at trying to prevent the government from importing cheaper anti-AIDS drugs, rape victims still can't get anti-retroviral drugs to prevent them from developing AIDS. Instead, doctors who have provided them with anti-retrovirals have been accused, by Mpumalanga's minister of health, of trying to overthrow the government.

The picture of our national minister of health, Dr Manto Tshabalala-Msimang, in the *New York Times*, jubilant after the decision by the pharmaceutical companies on 19 April, gave new hope. But for all that jubilation, AIDS patients have no advocates among elected officials.

One could say without exaggeration that the state's failure to face the facts about AIDS at the expense of human life is approaching criminal levels. In its failure to respond effectively, the government ignores principles that lie not only at the heart of leadership, but also at the heart of all humanity.

The first step towards a healthier path would be for leaders to publicly announce that there is a crisis, and that attitudes towards sex and sexual practices need to change. Gone are the 1960s and 1970s when sex was equal to adventure. Among other things, the practice of multiple sexual partners should be actively discouraged, and monogamous relationships encouraged. Who better to do this than political leaders themselves? 'We', Mr President, do have a problem of sexual promiscuity among our men. Ask any woman.

15. Unearthing private skeletons is another form of rape

Sunday Tribune, 19 March 2006

> *On 7 March 2006, the second day of Jacob Zuma's rape trial, the Johannesburg High Court allowed the complainant to be questioned about her sexual history, which is otherwise prohibited by Section 227 of the Criminal Procedures Act. Two days later, Zuma's lawyer, Kemp J Kemp produced the woman's memoirs, which revealed that she had been raped at the ages of 5, 13 and 14. I felt the Act was in place for the very purpose of protecting women against situations such as these, when women not only endure sexual violence, but are consequently disregarded because of their status as victims.[13]*

THE JACOB ZUMA rape trial transcends sexual politics, and is surpassed by broader issues such as responsible leadership, integrity, and the betrayal of trust. Zuma is the deputy president of South Africa's ruling party. He is a family man, and was, prior to the accusation of rape, the deputy president of the country. He was generally considered to be a peace-maker, a role model, and an advocate for what he termed 'the values and morals of nation-building'. His public show of bravado in the face of the details of the sexual act (whether it was rape or consensual sex) that took place in his home with a woman who is considered to be part of his family, and who is not his wife, and who regarded him as her father, is disturbing. In whatever direction the court decides on the rape trial, Zuma has put a dent in his integrity, and failed as a moral leader.

---

[13] *Mail & Guardian*, 'Timeline of the Jacob Zuma rape trial', 21 March 2006, http://mg.co.za/article/2006-03-21-timeline-of-the-jacob-zuma-rape-trial.

He knew every painful detail of the trauma suffered by the woman who calls him uncle, and as the father-figure he was expected to be after the death of the woman's own father, Zuma had a responsibility to protect her vulnerability. He had a responsibility to be faithful to his family. And he had a responsibility to live up to his reputation as a man of integrity, upholding the values and principles which he espoused when he led the Moral Regeneration Movement (MRM) and the National AIDS Council. He failed on all three.

At the first conference to launch the MRM in November 2004, Zuma described the new initiative as the most inspiring contribution to the efforts of building 'a caring, humane ethical society' in South Africa. The MRM, Zuma explained, was founded 'on the principles that South Africans are highly moral beings [who] are appalled by the symptoms of moral decay, which sometimes occur in our country'. He went on to list those symptoms of moral decay, which included the abuse of women, crime, and a lack of respect for others. Each of these symptoms of moral decay, however, has been enacted at Zuma's rape trial in various forms, both inside and outside the courtroom.

In whatever way one looks at the story told at Zuma's trial, a violation was committed. Sexual penetration by a parent or other adult who has power and authority over a younger family member is a betrayal, and an extreme violation of trust. There are three blows suffered by a woman who has experienced sexual violation. The penetration is the first blow; the denial that it happened – it was not what it seemed – is the second blow; to be blamed for the sexual crime is the third. There is a fourth blow for the woman with whom Zuma claims he had consensual sex: the private story of the traumas she had suffered at the hands of abusive men from an early age was scrutinised, dissected, and torn apart in public. When the court of justice and the court of public opinion had paraded her pain, her story was used to cast doubt on her mental state, her morality and her credibility. This was the 'second rape', and no doubt left her emotionally wounded. Bringing up women's past sexual history, especially if this is traumatic, should be forbidden, because it imposes an unjust burden on the women survivors of sexual abuse.

As I followed the reports on the Zuma trial, it occurred to me that the issue of sexism in our society is thriving, and that patriarchy in the courtroom should not be thrust aside. Rape trials, especially where the alleged rapist is a man of higher social status, are notoriously distressing for rape survivors. All too often women are stereotyped by the legal system, the media, the public, and sometimes family members, as the ones responsible for their own sexual assault by male relatives.

They are asked to prove they are not guilty of inviting the perpetrator's advances and precipitating the rape: their dress code, behaviour, and sexual history are routinely put under a microscope in what Caroline Taylor calls 'trial by ambush' in her book *Court Licensed Abuse*. If they did not scream, shout and scratch their assailant, they are blamed for having 'consented'. This view of consent ignores the fact that not all rape is violent. Some rapists, mostly those who rape women and children in the privacy of their homes, manipulate their victims into compliance.

Closely aligned with consent is the issue of choice. When women do not have the power to make a choice at all, they 'choose' silence. Abusive men have a way of fostering dependence, so that refusing their sexual advances is approached with fear – not fear of violence, but fear of loss of whatever it is that forms the basis of the dependency on the man. Yet women are haunted by shame when they realise that they should have fought the man's advances, although they know they could not at the time.

If, as Zuma claims, he had consensual sex with the complainant, it is he who should be shamed: for failure to control himself from having intercourse with his comrade's daughter who calls him uncle; for modelling destructive and inappropriate behaviour to young people by penetrating a woman without the use of a condom; for failure to publicly condemn what was done in his name by his supporters outside the courtroom, the slandering and stoning of his former comrade's daughter.

There is a thin line between the slandering of 'enemies' by angry crowds and violent murder; the 'necklace' murders that plunged many South African communities into a vortex of violence in the 1980s are still too fresh in memory. Zuma is playing with fire at the expense of many of those whose lives remain buried in the abyss of economic suffering. When he has finished, with his popularity 'intact', we might be left with an irreversible spiral of moral degeneration. At a time when South Africa needs leadership to guide its young generation and help them develop their sexuality with a healthy awareness of the risk of HIV and AIDS, Zuma has failed as a leader.

The Zuma trial should serve as a warning: the threat to women's rights may be entering a new era in South Africa. Sexism is deeply embedded in our society, and affects the way in which rape is treated by the public. On a continent where countless women and girls have been victims of rape in wars and in their homes, Zuma's rape trial gives us the opportunity to reflect on the threat that male power can pose to women in their own homes and communities.

Our constitution ushered in a decade of freedom, equity, and human rights laws. We have a National Gender Desk, a Women's Commission, and gender desks in many organs of civil society. This great record could lull us into a sense of complacency, but the questions that this trial raises are a harsh reminder that the time for complacency has not yet arrived.

16. What has happened to the ANC's morality?

THE WITNESS, 23 MAY 2006

Delivering judgment in Jacob Zuma's rape trial in the Johannesburg High Court on 8 May 2006, Judge Willem van der Merwe found it 'plausible' that Zuma, at age 63, had had consensual sex with a 31-year-old woman who called him 'Uncle'.[14] A week later, Zuma was reinstated as deputy president of the ANC despite public outrage over his statement in court that he had taken a shower to minimise the risk of contracting HIV from the complainant. The unquestioning political backing of his supporters speaks of political ambitions transcending a concern for the nation's greater good.[15]

WE LIVE IN a time of extraordinary possibilities. The barriers of the past are no longer cast in legal stone. We live in a society that is becoming increasingly inclusive. Democracy that came with the first all-race elections ushered in new freedoms which have created powerful channels of expression, freedoms previously denied to the majority of South Africans. Our constitution, lauded as one of the best in the world, has given us more than a decade of freedom, equity, and human rights laws.

Yet this is also a precarious time. The televised national seminar of Jacob Zuma's rape trial has focused our attention on the funda-

---

[14] While finding Zuma not guilty, the judge stated: 'I find it inexcusable that the accused would have unprotected sex with a woman so many years younger than him, who is the child of one of his comrades. That intercourse endangered her health and his.'

[15] BBC News, 'SA's Zuma "showered to avoid HIV"', 5 April 2006, http://news.bbc.co.uk/2/hi/africa/4879822.stm; *Mail & Guardian*, 'Zuma found not guilty', 8 May 2006, http://mg.co.za/article/2006-05-08-zuma-found-not-guilty; IOLnews, 'Zuma reinstated as ANC deputy president', 15 May 2006; A Meldrum, 'Acquitted Zuma ready to fight for presidency', *The Guardian*, 9 May 2006, http://www.theguardian.com/world/2006/may/09/southafrica.topstories3.

mental dilemma that is beginning to shape our nation's future: the dilemma of moral leadership. Zuma's return to the second highest position of leadership in the ANC is a terrible shame. At a time when we as a nation need leaders of moral character, there is little to celebrate. The 'we', of course, refers to us, 'the anonymous mass', as Njabulo Ndebele described those of us who fall outside the camp of both Zuma's supporters and the ANC.

The ANC, an organisation ahead of its time, with a vision to build a country where all who live in it shall have equal rights, an organisation that crafted the Freedom Charter which paved the way to our current constitution, was led by men and women whose moral character was our armour, men and women whose only ambition was to lead their country to freedom.

They pursued the quest for freedom vigorously and with resolve, risking danger, detention, torture, and even death. They dedicated their lives to the fight for equality, carried themselves with dignity, and fought to restore a spirit of shared humanity among all South Africans. This ambition and dedication to build a new society is captured most poignantly in the famous words of Nelson Mandela before he was sentenced to life imprisonment with his comrades.

The ideal of a democratic and free society, Mandela told the court, 'is an ideal which I hope to live for and to achieve. But if needs be, it is an ideal for which I am prepared to die.' These are the memorable words of Mandela to the court which pronounced a clear and unequivocal guilty verdict.

These were not just Mandela's words. They were the embodiment of the principles that formed the backbone of the ambition to free our country and to lead it on the road to humanity, freedom and equality. This ambition brought South Africans across colour and creed barriers to join with others and live their lives in a meaningful and dignified way, knowing that in making such a choice, they were risking the safety of their families, detention, torture and death.

Today, however, ambition among some in the leadership of the ANC has become a personal matter. It is ambition driven by self-interest, loyalties, party pressure, and a desire to be top dog. The big issues of nation-building and how to lead with dignity and style have taken a back seat. This is why Zuma, after he had disgraced himself in public with his lack of judgment and with a kind of behaviour that even the judge who handed him back his freedom considered to be deplorable, is now on a path that could advance his personal ambitions – to the highest position of political leadership in our country.

Zuma's supporters say it is enough that he has been found not guilty. 'Not guilty', however, is not the same as 'innocent'. Zuma knew every painful detail of the trauma suffered by his accuser, and after the death of her father, who was his comrade, Zuma had a responsibility to protect the vulnerable young woman. He had a responsibility to be faithful to his family. And he had a responsibility to live up to his reputation as a man of integrity, upholding the values and principles which he espoused when he led the Moral Regeneration Movement and the National AIDS Council. He failed on all three. Zuma has put a dent in his integrity, and failed as a moral leader.

Everything has been said about Zuma – his behaviour, his character, and his failure to publicly condemn the acts of violence done by his supporters to his former comrade's daughter. His supporters have evoked images of a man unfairly treated by conspirators within the ANC. The struggle is no longer about who is the best to lead South Africa into a future peaceful stability, but between the characters of two leaders (and why should it be a choice between these two? Are there no other choices?).

On the one hand there is Thabo Mbeki, seen as manipulative, intolerant of criticism, and out of touch with the masses while enjoying associations with important people internationally. However, Mbeki has also earned the respect of leaders at home and abroad as a visionary and a strategist, and for being strong on important domestic issues such as gender equality and issues that affect people with disabilities. On the other hand is Zuma, seen by many as warm, engaging, close to people, yet not strong on strategic vision.

Reinstating Zuma to his position as second in command of the ANC when his corruption trial is still unresolved, knowing that this places him in line for the presidential candidacy, raises questions about the ANC's motives. First, has the might of Zuma's supporters taken control of the ANC's wisdom on this issue? And second, is the ANC leadership motivated by fear of the firestorm they might ignite among furious Zuma supporters if Zuma were not reinstated?

The Zuma saga is as much about power and ambition as it is about the characters of Zuma and Mbeki. Unfortunately, we – 'the anonymous masses' – are at the mercy of the tyranny of the majority. Or are we? What can we do to uphold and advance Nelson Mandela's vision of a peaceful and cohesive society and Thabo Mbeki's vision of economic stability, and so give South Africa a global edge?

The challenge to us as engaged citizens, it seems to me, is to temper the right of different groups to express their dissatisfaction and outrage with moral wisdom. One wonders why ANC leaders of integrity, honesty, character, and regard for the respect and dignity of others have been silent – leaders like Nelson Mandela, Ahmed Kathrada, and Ben Turok, among many others. Where are their voices of reason in this crisis? Where are these leaders who pointed out for us the road to humaneness? And how can the next generation of moral leaders, whom they raised as their heirs, carry on and make their voices heard?

Clearly, our society needs to groom new, younger leaders. How do we cultivate them? Would it help to create a moral leadership forum involving schools in which moral development and leadership skills could be developed early, teaching the young how to use their power towards moral goals? Would it help to encourage leaders in the corporate sector and their employees to follow ethical codes of conduct, and to engage beyond the mandatory corporate social responsibility code?

Statements made in the press by many of Zuma's male followers in the Young Communist League, ANC Youth League and others are a frightening reminder of the power of misguided patriarchy among some of our younger leaders. David Masondo's words in the *Sunday Times* of 14 May are particularly troubling. Zuma, like any adult, Masondo said, 'has the right to have sex with any consenting adult – to argue that he should not be president because he had sex with an HIV-positive consenting adult is morally wrong.' Masondo is the national chairman of the Young Communist League. We should be worried, for two reasons among others. First, is sex going to become the yardstick for the selection of a morally and professionally qualified leader of our nation in the future South Africa? And second, what does consenting mean? Is consent determined by the judgment of a man in power?

What kind of morality is Masondo advocating? And, since we can reasonably assume that Masondo represents the next generation of ANC leaders, what hope do women have? The words of Alan Paton resonate in this crisis of leadership in our country: 'Cry, the beloved country, for the unborn [girl] child who will inherit our fear.'

17. Abuse of power through silencing dialogue

Mail & Guardian, 9 December 2008

In 2008, two professors at the University of KwaZulu-Natal, Nithaya Chetty and John van den Berg, were suspended for publicly criticising university management over issues of academic freedom.[16] Some commentators linked UKZN's policy of censure to racial transformation at the university. In this article, I sought to disentangle the core issues and the highly charged reactions.

ON THE WEBSITE of the National Tertiary Education Staff Union (NTESU), the number of signatures under the petition entitled 'Defending Academic Freedom at UKZN' are rising every hour. Browsing through the list, the names of academics and senior students are coming fast and furious from all the corners of the globe. Their voices, represented in the brief remarks submitted with their signatures, are loud and clear.

An academic from a university in Denmark comments: 'Freedom of critique – including critique of university management – is a core value of academic freedom.' Another from Brazil decries the abuse of power through silencing dialogue and debate in academic institutions, and calls it a 'continuation of apartheid

---

[16] Chetty and Van den Berg were charged with 'not exercising due care in communicating with the media' and bringing the university into disrepute. Van den Berg, a professor of mathematics, eventually signed a settlement agreement terminating disciplinary hearings against him, while Chetty, an associate professor and president of the SA Institute of Physics, elected to resign. The charges arose out of their criticisms of vice-chancellor Professor Malegapuru Makgoba's alleged attempts to prevent a faculty of Science and Agriculture submission on academic freedom from appearing on the senate agenda. Makgoba banned academics and staff from meeting to discuss the disciplinary action against the professors. See Wikipedia, Controversies at the University of KwaZulu-Natal, http://en.wikipedia. org/wiki/Controversies_at_the_University_of_KwaZulu-Natal.

practices under a different name'. A professor from The Hague expresses concern that events at UKZN are a reversal of the democratic gains splendidly reflected in the South African constitution, and threaten a 'move in the direction of authoritarianism'. From India, Thailand, Canada, Malawi, the United Kingdom, the United States, and our own shores, the news of UKZN management's treatment of Professors Nithaya Chetty and John van den Berg has stirred academics across the globe.

The story of these two professors and the disciplinary fate that awaits them, however, is just the tip of the iceberg of the politics of power at universities. Their experiences have echoes not only in other academic institutions across the country, but also in schools, courts, government, churches, media institutions and the corporate sector. The abuse of power in many of our institutions resembles, in subtle ways, the abuses we have witnessed in government, both our own and our regional neighbours' governments. There are stories of abuses of power in other liberal institutions that would shock readers if they were disclosed in this newspaper.

One finds that when people have been in positions of power in academic institutions for too long, they are sometimes caught up in rigid bureaucratic styles where the only rule that matters is obedience to authority. A spirit of dialogue among colleagues is stifled. In such an atmosphere, rules serve the purpose of erecting a form of authoritarian control, where action is directed by the priority placed on people to do their 'duty' uncritically and unquestioningly. Those who dare to speak out on issues of principle are either ignored or immediately silenced without a hearing. And if they persist, they may be punished in a range of ways that are sugar-coated with appropriate language aimed at concealing the element of punishment. Such a leadership style destroys freedom systematically, but very subtly, while introducing fear.

What surprises me the most about the story of Chetty and Van den Berg is that for all the structures that universities have set up to protect their members against discrimination and abuses of power, structures presumably aimed at resolving internal matters amicably, Chetty and Van den Berg have had to 'go public' with their struggles. This is an indictment not only of senior management, but also of all those who walk the corridors of power at UKZN. This, in my view, is the important aspect. If those in positions of leadership at universities cannot show the courage to stand in the eye of the proverbial storm and to chart the path toward change, what hope do we have for transformation at these institutions?

Transformation must include transforming the meaning of power and leadership in institutions of higher learning. There are moments when senior academics who serve in leadership roles have to show courage, and bare their moral stature. In the best of these moments, these leaders will step in to raise their voices about important matters of principle, and thus will raise the debate to a higher level. Elie Wiesel's statement 'to remain silent and indifferent is the greatest sin of all' should be the mantra for all of us, but especially for those in positions of leadership. Power and authority in an environment that nurtures critical thinking and independence cannot simply be about issuing orders, and expecting silence and uncritical obedience.

Institutions of higher learning are required to contribute meaningfully to a new society. I doubt that there is any university today without an institutional transformation programme. Unfortunately, 'transformation' at universities has focused too narrowly on race and gender, an agenda driven mainly by changing the face of our institutions by placing more women, blacks, and coloured people in positions of leadership. Very rarely do questions about the moral stature and integrity of those appointed form part of appointment decisions. Therefore, we find that little is changing in academic institutions.

Granted, there are many reasons for this: anti-transformation elites who find sophisticated ways of blocking the transformation goals of their institutions; those who push transformation as a law to be enforced, resulting in inevitable resistance; those who feel threatened by change and are simply afraid of facing an unknown future; and numerous others. We cannot know with certainty what passions, fears and/or demons are raging in the hearts of our fellow human beings. However, I believe that if we can create a collegiate environment that encourages dialogue in our institutions instead of silencing it, we can learn to respect one another, and treat each other with dignity.

Some of the problems we have witnessed in institutions around the country are part of the larger context of our search for identity in a changing society. They have to do with our deepest and most hidden fears about what it means to be white, and what it means to be coloured or black in our changing institutions. These issues require a much more thoughtful debate, and a mutually respectful dialogue. The test of progress in our academic institutions will be measured by our ability to learn to talk to one another and really listen to others who may be different from us. Diversity in our institutions is even more vital now than it has been in the past. However, much more is needed.

The call to defend academic freedom should really be a call to dialogue about how to foster compassionate leadership in our institutions; leadership inspired by the desire to empower others to become better human beings. All around us we see the imperfections of our young democracy and the frailty of human justice. We can learn from these examples and take stock in the tradition of Socratic reflection by reflecting continually on our actions, and continually questioning the decisions we make in our different roles at various levels of leadership in the institutions in which we serve.

18. Zuma should lead instead of spreading fear

Mail & Guardian, 24 April 2009

On 6 April 2009, the National Prosecuting Authority decided to drop charges of corruption, fraud and money-laundering against former vice-president Jacob Zuma. In speeches to his supporters during the trial, Zuma invoked the language of struggle and warfare. By branding the court as 'the enemy', Zuma effectively ushered in an era of censure of criticism against him. In this article, I tried to put this pivotal moment into perspective.

THERE HAVE BEEN moments when our leaders have faced challenges that have called upon them to lead with moral vision. At their best, in addressing the matter at hand, the leaders have put their country first, and made choices that transcend personal ambition. Nelson Mandela immediately comes to mind. His response to the assassination of Chris Hani was to implore black and white South Africans to unite. Looking grave and sad, he called for calm 'from the very depths of my being'. I recall witnessing the fear in white motorists' faces when mourners travelling to Hani's funeral poured out of minibuses that had stopped at a petrol station in Welkom. There was anger and rage in the air, but there was also restraint.

The essence of Mandela's leadership was moral authority, and a keen awareness of the potential for violence and destructiveness in our society. In a country with a history of violent anti-apartheid protests, systematic abuses of power by the apartheid government, and state-sanctioned violence against those perceived to be enemies of the state, Mandela recognised his role in building a culture of tolerance. He understood clearly that mobilising crowds of supporters had to be done with caution.

What we have witnessed over the past couple of years during Zuma's court appearances, however, is in contrast to this cautionary principle. The speeches delivered to crowds mobilised at Zuma's court appearances have conveyed a spirit of protest that has permeated many sectors of civil society, rupturing the sense of responsible citizenship among some ANC members entrusted with authority in institutions such as schools.

Unfortunately, the NPA's decision not to prosecute Zuma has resulted in the blurring of the distinction between the corruption charges against him on the one hand, and the alleged political meddling by Thabo Mbeki and his cohorts in the NPA on the other. Thus, the corruption charges saga may not be over yet.

The dark cloud of unanswered corruption charges hanging over Zuma's head has been redefined as a figment of his enemies' imagination. There is no cloud, Zuma's strategists have claimed. The message conveyed to Zuma's supporters – successfully, it seems – is that his enemies are out to get him. It is this 'enemy' language aimed at silencing questions voiced by concerned citizens about a future president who, for whatever reason, has not addressed corruption charges against him, that concerns me.

Harsh statements and actions that border on inciting violence in response to Zuma's critics are not new. Not surprisingly, when these very actions were repeated by other organisations, such as the defacing of a poster with Zuma's picture in KwaZulu-Natal, the ANC leadership immediately protested that these were signs of intolerance and disrespect for their leader. Yet several instances of the burning of Mbeki's image – while he was still president – outside the courts where Zuma was appearing were met with silence from the leaders of the ANC and its alliance partners. The message conveyed by such silence seems to be the following: the destructive actions of our own members are justified as long as they target our enemies, but we will condemn similar actions by our enemies. The silence speaks louder than words, and breeds a political culture in which the thresholds of intolerance begin to sink lower and lower.

Recently, while attending the 15th anniversary of the genocide in Rwanda, I was reminded of the devastating consequences of the language of intolerance which stirs up hatred against individuals and groups perceived to be in the enemy camp. This week I am in Berlin to speak at a conference on reconciliation organised by the University of Jena. I was reminded again of how leaders in Germany mobilised crowds of supporters to sow seeds of hatred.

The progression to acts of violence against individuals perceived as enemies begins with the demonisation of those individuals and the groups to which they belong. Examples of this phenomenon are emerging as the elections draw near. The violent clash between Mbeki and Zuma supporters at the ANC's Limpopo Elective Conference last year, which led to the killing of two ANC members, is a troubling echo from the past. A recent remark by Julius Malema that Helen Zille's dancing with members of her party at an election campaign rally reminds him of an apartheid-era spy carries the same innuendo as his 'kill for Zuma' statement.

Having spent many hours in the past interviewing perpetrators of apartheid atrocities, necklace murders, and other gross human rights violations, I have learnt how easy it is for ordinary human beings to be stirred into acts of violence by public statements made by their leaders. The trend of political intolerance reflected in the public speeches of prominent leaders of the ANC alliance partners should be named for what it is: it is dangerous, and it threatens a return to the politics of hate and violence that characterised political life in South Africa during the reign of the apartheid government, as well as the complexities of the anti-apartheid struggle in the past.

At its worst, the violent intolerance of the anti-apartheid struggle was epitomised by the 'necklace' murders of comrades, friends and neighbours at the slightest suspicion that they were police spies. That is a past we remember with a feeling of shame, and a sense that a lot was lost that could have been prevented. At the same time, for many South Africans the past represents the hard-fought years of the anti-apartheid revolution. Zuma, Mbeki, Mandela and others fought hard and led us to the dawn of a new era, to this, our proud democracy.

To cast Zuma's battles to rid himself of the corruption charges against him as the new revolution, and anybody who disagrees with this stance as 'counter-revolutionary', shifts the focus away from the real work of restoring dignity to the majority of our people, and strengthening our democracy. Now that evidence of political meddling has been revealed, what remains unaddressed for many South Africans is where our future president stands regarding the charges of corruption against him. In a government that has been riddled with stories of widespread corruption from the top leadership to the lowest level of civil servants, it is our right as citizens to know, and for Zuma to address this issue of corruption charges. Sadly, this is a subject that Zuma and the ANC leadership want to forget. It is *'finish en klaar'* (done and dusted), according to Lindiwe Sisulu.

Those who speak out are attacked with threats, as we found out from recent reports that veterans of the ANC's Umkhonto weSizwe have threatened war if DA leader Helen Zille pursues the legal route to get Jacob Zuma to face his corruption charges.

Archbishop Desmond Tutu, stalwart of the global fight for social justice and for years the thorn in the flesh of the apartheid government in the struggle for freedom in our own country, has been labelled by Zizi Kodwa of the ANC as part of a 'lynch mob' mobilised to discredit Zuma.

How quickly we backslide. Under the apartheid government the voice of dissent was silenced. Courageous people, among them Archbishop Tutu, were unstoppable. Times change; it is now 2009. A black government led by people who fought fearlessly against apartheid is in power. Yet somehow things stay the same. Today Archbishop Tutu is demonised and portrayed as part of a 'lynch mob' unleashed to destroy Jacob Zuma.

There is no longer an apartheid government that seeks to silence its opponents with oppressive laws and with murder. Rather, the threats come from the ANC and its alliance partners, spreading fear in order to silence citizens' rights to question those in positions of leadership. The ANC, and the future president of our country, would do well to shift gears and to focus attention on uniting the people of our beautiful country. Fifteen years after the birth of freedom and democracy, this is an extraordinary moment to change history and to avoid South Africa deteriorating into a statistic of the African continent, where corruption and violence reign under post-colonial governments.

Mamphela Ramphele has observed that hospitals across the country are in a shameful state. This is borne out, among other factors, by the increasing number of deaths of babies and/or mothers during birth. Criticism can only strengthen our leaders. The ANC has a right to celebrate its achievements of the past 15 years. More importantly, however, it should face its failures. It should work for real change in the lives of many South Africans, and be an effective government that will finally deliver on its promise of change. Jacob Zuma should rise to this challenge and to this profound moment in our history, and lead us to the great vision that he fought for. It is the only way to bring change and lasting peace to our country.

19. Not all is well with Zuma's soul

Mail & Guardian, 19 October 2012

On 4 August 2012, the ANC Women's League used the Fifth Charlotte Maxeke Annual Memorial Lecture held in Bloemfontein as a vehicle for expressing its uncritical adulation of President Jacob Zuma. Toubled by what I witnessed both inside and outside the lecture venue, I reflected on the growing moral crisis in our country, and what we need to do to surmount it.

LAST SUNDAY I attended a service at the Park Avenue Methodist Church in New York. The sermon, by the Reverend Cathy Gilliard, was based on the story of the orphaned Jewish girl Esther who was chosen to be the queen of Persia. When the king's right-hand man devised a plot to kill all the Jewish people because Esther's uncle, Mordecai, refused to bow down to him, Esther continued to hide her identity. But Mordecai called on Esther to stop playing it safe and speak out on behalf of her people: 'Who knows? Perhaps you have come to royal dignity for just such a time as this.' It is a poignant story that reminds us of the moral responsibility to speak out against injustice and corruption.

As I listened to Gilliard's sermon, I recalled another woman's voice – one that has plagued me since the launch of this year's 'women's month' at the University of the Free State. It was the voice of a member of the ANC Women's League, hero-worshipping President Jacob Zuma.

The occasion was the fifth annual Charlotte Maxeke memorial lecture. If you were at the university that day, you would have been forgiven for thinking there was a film crew there, re-enacting apartheid-era scenes of police violence. The large police van and other police vehicles parked on the perimeter of the Callie Human

Centre, where Zuma was to deliver the lecture, ominously resembled a scene from the past.

Inside the large hall, the scene was just as gloomy. Police in 'riot uniform', hands on their rifles, paraded along the upper level above the stage. At strategic points and on the steps leading to the upper level, to the right and left of the stage where Zuma was sitting, conspicuously young-looking soldiers in camouflage gear and maroon berets were standing watch in pairs, unarmed, or at least with no visible firearms. These young soldiers were not the apartheid government's army of conscripts about to be deployed to 'the border' or 'the townships'. The armed police on the upper level were not to be mistaken for apartheid police, who were quick to shoot black demonstrators. Or that is what I thought until the 'script' of the military forces around the president in the hall was playing out.

The Free State ANC Women's League had organised the event to honour the memory of Maxeke, but this script was not about her legacy. It was, rather, a chance for the league to show its adoration of the president. Every detail of the event was orchestrated as a build-up to his speech, which he delivered by reading Maxeke's biography. Nkosazana Dlamini-Zuma, recently elected as the first woman to lead the African Union, would have delivered a more profound message, but was only given time to 'say a few words'. This was Zuma's day; his day of being celebrated by the league. The league member chairing the event came on stage to tell the audience that the president would be entering the hall soon, and there had to be absolute silence when he walked in.

We were given candles, which I thought represented the light Maxeke shone selflessly to open the way for the formidable women's movement against injustice. But a different purpose for the candles was soon revealed. Volunteers went round the hall, lighting the candles. 'Shhhhh, shhhhh,' the chairperson implored the restless audience. 'There should be no noise when the president enters the hall. The lights will be turned off and only the sound of the burning candles should be heard,' she said.

As we waited, burning candles in hand, several announcements about the imminent entry of the president were made. Watching this theatre and listening to the chairperson telling us about the 'forces of evil' raging outside (a reference to the anti-Zuma songs being sung outside the hall), and urging us to 'pray for our president', it struck me that the league no longer embodied the spirit of the noble fight against the injustices suffered by marginalised women.

In post-apartheid South Africa, the league has lost the moral freedom that defined it in the past, when it was driven by a desire to widen the horizons of possibility for women of colour in our country. Today's league is more concerned with fighting to save Zuma's political career or the careers of members' comrades.

An uncritical 'love' for Zuma was unmistakable in the music performed that day. At first, the songs were a mixture of light dance and choral music with no real significance. But the music changed when Zuma approached the hall, giving symbolic meaning to the quest to save his political career by fighting the 'enemy' – the voices of dissent. As Zuma's procession entered the hall, a talented young trio sang the words from Puccini's 'Nessun Dorma' aria, often used at World Cup ceremonies as an emphatic statement of victory: '*Vincerò! Vincerò! Vincerò!*' (I shall win!). This orchestrated symbolic statement glossed over the fact that, in the opera 'Turandot', the promised *vincerò* comes only after an act of mass death. Thus, in the terrain of the symbolic imagination, we might consider that, as Zuma's bid for another presidential term moves towards victory, there may be destruction along the way. Hence the importance of the prayers for which the league pleaded: 'Please pray for our president.'

This prayer component was captured by the song 'It is Well with My Soul', sung by the gospel singer Sechaba just before Zuma came to the podium. The song's original meaning conveys an unwavering trust in God in the face of life's challenges.

Listening to Sechaba's voice booming through the hall with so much power and emotion, and watching him projected on the large screen in front, I was left breathless. There was Sechaba performing on the screen, in a pink golf shirt and khaki pants, singing 'It is well with my soul' with joy on his face, while at the same time passing back and forth in front of two young 'soldiers' in camouflage uniform, wearing maroon berets and standing at attention, stern-faced and hard-mouthed. One saw then that in reality Zuma does not put his trust only in God, and that all is not well with the president's soul.

These images made a deep impression on me. The scripts created collectively by the ANC and its alliance partners since the days of Zuma's legal battles – scripts created to save him from rape and corruption charges – have played out in a ceaseless spiral. From the public dramas around Julius Malema to Bheki Cele's militarisation of the police, from the Marikana massacre and the arrest of student Chumani Maxwele for allegedly giving Zuma the middle finger, from the killing of Andries Tatane during a protest in Ficksburg, to the looting of public funds to transform Zuma's homestead into a palace complex, all these point to the crisis of moral leadership in our country.

It is a gruesome tale – how we have moved so rapidly from the era of hope to the bleak landscape ushered in by Zuma's ascent to power, how we find ourselves in a state characterised by poor service delivery, major corruption at all levels of government, increasing violence against women, and many other problems that have torn apart the moral fibre of our society.

What can it all mean? What if it all comes down to this, that at such a time we are all called to step up, as Esther did when she saw the destruction about to befall her people? 'When we remember who we are,' Gilliard said at the New York church, 'when we stand at the intersection where potential meets necessity and necessity meets possibility – and we all will stand there at some point in our lives – we stand there and search ourselves. At best, we refuse, absolutely refuse, to live beneath our potential.' We choose, instead, to be courageous, to interrupt the spiral into the tragic dramas playing out in our communities.

How I wish the voice of the ANC Women's League could be restored to that courageous place. How I pray for South African citizens to march in step on the path that leads to hope – hope that South Africa can regain the dignity it had at the birth of our democracy.

20. Zuma has corrupted the soul of South Africa

Mail & Guardian, 24 May 2013

> *In a recent interview with* The Guardian, *the Zambian vice-president, Guy Scott, compared President Jacob Zuma to the National Party's last leader, FW de Klerk, saying: 'He's very like De Klerk. He tells us, "You just leave Zimbabwe to me." Excuse me, who the hell liberated you anyway? Was it not us?'[17] This gibe, implying that Zuma is arrogant and conceited, only scratches the surface of the ANC's current failure to provide moral leadership to a nation at a crucial time.*

THE RECENT COMMENT by the Zambian vice-president, Guy Scott, likening President Jacob Zuma to former president FW de Klerk is unfair to De Klerk. At a critical moment in South African politics, De Klerk listened to the voices that called for change.

He was not blind to the unpalatable reality that it was time for apartheid to go – whatever pressures prevailed to 'force' him, as some might say, to release Nelson Mandela in February 1990, and to use his power to call a referendum in March 1992 to determine the support of white voters for political negotiations. De Klerk could have ignored wise counsel and dug in his heels – like his predecessor, PW Botha.

---

[17] The outspoken Scott also said: 'The South Africans are very backward in terms of historical development. I hate South Africans. That's not a fair thing to say, because I like a lot of South Africans, but they really think they're the bees' knees and actually they've been the cause of so much trouble in this part of the world. I have a suspicion the blacks model themselves on the whites now that they're in power. "Don't you know who we are, man?"' David Smith, 'Zambian vice-president: "South Africans are backward"', *The Guardian*, 1 May 2013, http://www.theguardian.com/world/2013/may/01/zambian-vicepresident-south-africans-backward.

By contrast, Zuma relentlessly ignores warnings about consequences that are apparent to others. It is like the proverbial writing on the wall – a man entangled in a network of associations from which either he or his family benefits, blind to the potential negative impact that these relationships might have on his office as president of the country.

From the very beginning, Zuma's presidency was destined to corrupt the soul of the country. The dramas that unfolded during his court trials and after his acquittal have been burnt into our collective consciousness. Among these were members of the South African Democratic Teachers' Union abandoning pupils in the middle of examinations in order to join other Zuma supporters during his trial; scenes of aggressive protest against the young woman who accused Zuma of rape; the extraordinary admission by Zuma inside the courtroom that he had had unprotected sex and had taken a shower to minimise the risk of HIV infection; and Julius Malema leading the crowds of Zuma supporters and threatening to 'kill for Zuma' if he were not acquitted. These were disturbing images and, in my view, laid the foundation for what Zuma has called the 'moral decay' that has gripped our country.

Recently, the problem of violence in South African society has been discussed in numerous forums around the country, on radio, at institutions of higher learning, and by civil society organisations. The president also had his own initiative related to this matter, calling on religious leaders to help address this problem. Yet the 'moral rot' – to invoke Zuma once again – is in plain sight in the ANC's echelons of power. It is exemplified in the multiple extramarital love affairs of some of the most senior members of the ANC (and children born from some of these affairs); the gory details of allegations of physical and emotional abuse of a spouse and workers by a cabinet minister in the ANC government; the rampant corruption scandals involving ANC officials, from the highest level of leadership in government to the very lowest in provincial offices and at the country's border posts; and the assassination of ANC provincial leaders, and/or allegations of ANC leaders hiring hitmen to murder their opponents or those threatening to expose corruption.

Moral rot at the top can breed a lack of trust in government, disillusionment, and chaos, but wise leaders with moral stature bring stability – to paraphrase a biblical text. The cruellest of all features of Zuma's presidency is the continuing injustice of the failure of service delivery, the collapse of health institutions, and the dire state of many schools. All this cuts to the core of the soul of our country, rupturing the very essence of our being as a nation.

It is not surprising that we have now descended to the level of our young raping our old. These young people who are raping their grandmothers are not the 'lost generation' of apartheid; they are the 'born frees' of the new South Africa. They were promised a future that would open up into an horizon of hope and opportunity. Instead, they have become disenchanted, waking up daily to the yawning void of emptiness. Very few of them will escape the fate of intergenerational poverty in their homes and communities. Worse, the conditions under which many of our young people grow up are irreconcilable with the promises of change under the ANC government.

Under Zuma, our government seems to be edging inevitably closer to becoming a government of broken promises, corruption and unaccountability. Who can forget the shocking images in this newspaper of the appalling conditions at some schools in the Eastern Cape? If children are treated as if their lives do not count, they are likely to grow up with very little or no pride in their identity, and a sense of worthlessness. If they grow up feeling that their lives do not count, that they do not matter in the larger scheme of things, how can they be expected to bestow a sense of worth on others?

The life circumstances of marginalised young people in our country are similar to those of their parents and grandparents under apartheid – except that they are worse off than their forebears. Their parents and grandparents, relegated to second- and even third-class citizenship, 'expected' the apartheid government to treat them inhumanely. In this democracy of ours, however, many young people feel a deep sense of betrayal by a government they trusted. The broken promises of politicians, who seem more concerned about winning elections than about delivering on their promises, is a pain that cuts very deep, and explodes many young people's sense of hope. At the same time, as witnesses to the excesses of political elites and their business partners, they see that ours is a democracy that has benefited corrupt officials, the president, his family, and those with close ties to the president.

This culture of patronage – you scratch my back and I scratch yours – has defined the ANC's leadership over the past few years. It was epitomised most dazzlingly in Malema's rapid accumulation of wealth, and his shameless use of the coffers of a province as his private bank account. The brazen flaunting of this ill-gotten wealth by Malema when he was still protected by his close ties with Zuma reflects the kind of impunity that permeates the entire system.

This brazen display of disregard continues, as exemplified in the Gupta family's breach of national security at Waterkloof. Like the silence that repeatedly followed Malema's outrageous public statements, Zuma's deafening silence and failure to publicly condemn the Guptas for overstepping the limits of their relationship with him as head of state speaks louder than words. Why doesn't Zuma see the contradiction between this entanglement with the Guptas and his position? It seems clear that the president's permission was not sought for the Gupta's plane to land at Waterkloof; however, the hypocrisy of emphatic statements from senior government officials trying to distance the president from the actions of the Guptas was not lost on some observers of this saga.

This collective response from the top brass of the ANC government reminds me of FW de Klerk's attempt to distance himself from Eugene de Kock, the most highly decorated officer under apartheid, who headed the anti-insurgency unit stationed at Vlakplaas. The comparison may seem extreme. However, there is an unwritten agreement among political elites that when they feel ashamed because behaviour which they sanction in private has become public, the person responsible for the behaviour should not under any circumstances be portrayed as reasonable.

De Klerk, for example, has always suggested that De Kock was one of the bad apples of the apartheid security apparatus. If De Kock is a 'bad apple', then we need not look any further; the matter has been explained. On the other hand, the more we humanise him, the more we are forced to conclude that there were factors that led him to do what he did. One must then ask, what were those factors? And that is the fear from which the more guilt-ridden layers of those in power, the politicians and social elites who could have wielded influence, try to shield themselves.

To echo Zambia's Scott, like it or not, in very subtle and not so subtle ways, there are parallels between the way in which apartheid leaders used power as a system of social control and the strategic ways in which the ANC uses its power.

21. ANC's 'treason' cry a repressive apartheid tactic

Mail & Guardian, 8 February 2013

In January 2013, First National Bank launched a brand campaign called 'You Can Help', featuring a series of online videos in which young people shared their views about South Africa and its future.[18] The ANC condemned the campaign as an 'attack on the president, his ministers, and government as a whole', and an ANC Youth League spokesperson declared it 'bordered on treason'.[19] This prompted me to argue that, at a time of increasing threats to our democracy, it was more important than ever to create spaces for the voices of young people.

THESE PAST FEW years have unsettled the boundaries of our fledgling democracy. Some of the challenges, such as the tendency of the ruling party to respond to healthy criticism with hostility, emerged during Thabo Mbeki's time as president. They became more pronounced after the election of President Jacob Zuma, a man whose various indiscretions are an open secret.

Some may say that these indiscretions are 'insignificant acts' in the larger scheme of the macropolitical realm, and that, in any case, the president apologised for some of them. Indeed, in the minds of some South Africans, these public apologies – for having unprotected sex with the woman who accused him of rape, for

---

[18] Most of the participants spoke frankly about South Africa's problems, ranging from unemployment to corruption and high rates of violence and crime.

[19] See *Politicsweb*, 'FNB's You Can Help campaign treasonous – ANCYL', 21 January 2013, http://www.politicsweb.co.za/politicsweb/view/politicsweb/en/page71654?oid=351747&sn=Detail; *Mail & Guardian*, 'ANC tears into FNB over "political statement"', 21 January 2013, http://mg.co.za/article/2013-01-21-00-anc-tears-into-fnb-over-brand-campaign/; *Business Day Live*, 'ANC outrage over FNB's "Arab Spring" ad campaign', 22 January 2013.

extramarital infidelity, and for his homophobic statement (gay and lesbian South Africans are a 'disgrace to the nation and to God') – loom larger on the horizon of the president's legacy than his exceptional leadership.

There is much at stake in our young democracy. Such 'insignificant acts' of the politically powerful often filter down to everyday social life, where they are emulated as 'codes of conduct' by many young people who look up to their leaders. If the statements of the leadership in the ruling party and its alliance partners embodied principles of democracy, they would be more likely to inspire the transformative social and economic vision that was our hope when apartheid collapsed.

The reaction by the ANC leadership and its alliance partners to the voices of young people posted on an FNB website as part of its 'You Can Help' campaign is troubling. To suggest that an act of agency – freedom of expression – is treasonable simply because it shines a critical spotlight on the government is a profound contradiction of the very essence of our democracy. Closing the space of dialogue in our society harks back to the bleakest days of the apartheid state's repressive policies.

A few years ago, I was part of a group that organised a public dialogue called 'Voices, Visions and Hopes of Our Youth: What's Missing in Our Democracy'. The event was inspired by the words of former President Nelson Mandela: 'When you invest in the youth, you invest in the future.' Five high-school students on the panel in a packed auditorium were invited to share the challenges they faced as young South Africans, and their hopes for the future. They came from public schools in Khayelitsha and Athlone, and private girls' schools in Cape Town and Durban.

We organised the event as an 'intergenerational' dialogue: the older generation comprised the political activist, educationalist and business leader Dr Mamphela Ramphele; the former minister of finance, Trevor Manuel; and the former deputy chairperson of the Truth and Reconciliation Commission, Dr Alex Boraine. I mention this event because of the enduring importance of the voices of these young people who spoke about a range of issues, including the failure of black economic empowerment to trickle down to communities with the greatest need, the slow pace of change, the lack of inspiration or vision in political campaigns, and violence and the lack of resources in schools.

The voices of two of the young people from Khayelitsha seem particularly significant to me now. One of them, a young woman in Grade 10, spoke about how threatening life was for gay and lesbian youths, especially girls, who often faced ridicule and the threat of 'corrective' rape at school and in their neighbourhood. The second, a student in Grade 11, spoke about the lack of security at school and the feelings of vulnerability that made it challenging to attend. He was a physical science student. With marks in the range of 60%-65%, he was confident that he would pass matric, but was concerned about whether he would be able to achieve his dream of studying at university, for two reasons: first, he had never seen a laboratory; and, second, the constant eruptions of violence at his school were beginning to erode his sense of hope.

I was reminded of the voices of these young people last week, and wondered how their lives had unfolded after their participation in our public dialogue a few years ago. The young woman from the private girls' school in Rondebosch, Cape Town, has graduated *cum laude* from a university in Cape Town, and the one from Durban is studying at a university in Johannesburg. Sadly, but unsurprisingly, given the dire circumstances of their schools and communities, the two young people from Khayelitsha have 'dropped out' of school. The young man was 'sent' to Gauteng by his family to find work, and the young woman returned to the Eastern Cape without completing high school. The challenges experienced by these young people – unsafe communities and unsafe schools, poor resources, poverty, inequality and unemployment – are played out from generation to generation.

When young people recently spoke about their experiences and expressed their views about what should be done, why were the ANC and its alliance partners so quick to appropriate the apartheid-era strategy of instilling fear and silencing dissent with allegations of treason? At this time of increasing threats to our democracy, and when governments in the developing world are advocating the importance of the voices of young people, the need for dialogue and opening a space for these voices is more vital than ever.

Silence young people, and they will emerge in powerful ways that can no longer be silenced. We already see this picture on national television. The lessons of the past are that rubber bullets and teargas cannot silence the hunger for change. Dialogue does so, creating the space for people to voice their unhappiness in order to chart a way forward towards a more stable country, a more stable democracy. It worked once, and it can work again.

Even more important is a need for reflection on the crisis of moral leadership in our country. Professor Barney Pityana spoke poignantly about this issue at the University of the Free State in December last year: 'Our leaders should not be separated from us, but should give us a vision of a better tomorrow.' It is possible for things to change for the better, he said, citing the changes that have taken place at the University of the Free State under Professor Jonathan Jansen's leadership.

Pityana pointed out that at the heart of the problem with the ANC's leadership was the notion that the 'collective' would decide.

Leadership matters, and so does taking responsibility. 'We no longer have a shared value and concern about the country,' he said. 'We can no longer believe that, even when we vote, democracy no longer means anything. We need to recover a fresh sense of democracy.'

The need for a fresh sense of democracy is why I believe Dr Mamphela Ramphele's (re)entry onto the political stage offers such promise. It is a promise to rebuild a space for moral engagement. We need to rebuild our nation, not because, as the president remarked at a church in KwaZulu-Natal last April, currently 'we have a nation of thugs'. Rather, we need to restore the morality that inspired the movement and the struggle for change in our country.

Legacies are unpredictable. President Zuma's legacy, it seems, is already written in the complicated narratives that ushered him into the presidency and in the narratives that have unfolded since. It is time to recover a fresh sense of democracy that will open the space for healthy exchange among all South Africans.

22. The bar is too high for SA's inept leaders

Mail & Guardian, 22 November 2013

Following the formation of the Economic Freedom Fighters, Julius Malema was compared with Thomas Isidore Sankara, the 'Che Guevara of Africa', who steered Burkina Faso away from the destructive legacy of colonialism. In this article, I agreed with Malema that South Africa needs a new breed of leaders – but concluded that he was no Sankara.

THERE IS NO reason to dispute what Julius Malema has been saying since re-entering the political stage: that our country needs a new breed of leaders. Nor is there any doubt about the role that his party, the Economic Freedom Fighters (EFF), is playing as one of the parties trying to occupy the emerging political space. After almost 20 years of democracy, the promise of a better life for all has not materialised for the majority of South Africans, many of them the generation of young people who never experienced the oppressive and discriminatory policies of apartheid directly.

Yet most of these young people face multiple disadvantages, in some cases worse than those faced by their parents' generation. They are trapped in a cycle of poor housing conditions, low income and poverty. There is widespread unemployment, the health and education systems in many towns and villages are in a deplorable state, and the chasm between rich and poor has deepened.

In countless South African communities, the post-apartheid democracy has not produced the opportunities and social outcomes it promised. Whether one can assume from Malema's impassioned rhetoric about economic freedom that he is the one to make social justice a reality for the majority of South Africans is left to one's imagination. In the absence of much evidence of Malema helping the poor when he was leader of the ANC Youth League, however, it would require a great leap of the imagination to predict how he will be transformed into a politician ready to channel farms and financial resources to the people first.

The bar has been set very high for Malema. He has been compared with Thomas Isidore Sankara, the man known as the 'Che Guevara of Africa'. In four years as president of the country he named Burkina Faso ('land of upright people'), he steered it away from the destructive legacy of colonialism. But Malema is no Sankara. Among the causes he championed in his four years as one of the most powerful leaders of the youth league – and the ANC itself – was the election of President Jacob Zuma. As Malema leads the EFF on the road to the 'riches' of political leadership, he is caught up in corruption charges.

The comparison with Sankara demands a great imaginative effort. On the face of it – the red beret, the brilliant rhetoric of economic freedom – Malema seems to be the living embodiment of both the hope Sankara evoked in his people, and his substantive achievements. But can Malema convert rhetoric into the real change that many of his young (and old) followers are hoping for? If elected, would he be able to transform himself from being a member of the class of 'those who stole from us … while the people continue to suffer' (as Andile Mngxitama put it in an open letter to him in *The Sowetan* in July 2011) into a benevolent politician for whom voters come first? Would he no longer be the author of the kind of self-serving excesses we saw during his leadership of the youth league?

Recently I was in Rwanda, travelling with one of my students. She was interviewing women in the Rwandan parliament for a postgraduate degree on women's leadership in the aftermath of genocide and mass violence. I went there to explore how Rwanda might produce a countervailing narrative on genocide, drawing on the rich research opening up there. In our encounter with government ministers, what struck me was that one could tell what was most important to them not only by what they were telling us but also by how they behaved. The first thing you noticed was the absence of flashy cars and bodyguards around these ministers. Even the official vehicles outside our hotel, where the country's president was speaking at a conference, were all Toyotas.

Contrast this with South Africa and the bling lifestyle of our leaders. In the narcissistic quest for the material pleasures of political position, seemingly pursued at any cost, some politicians' time and energy is directed at looking out for themselves rather than paying careful attention to how their behaviour affects the people who voted for them. South Africans who have not tasted the fruits of democracy see this, and experience it with a deep sense of betrayal.

To use 'the Boers' as a bogeyman, as Cyril Ramaphosa did recently on the ANC campaign trail, is to insult people's intelligence. When they have faced bitter disappointment and feel used, people look for evidence of hope to help them to get out of the trap of their connection to the governing political party that has let them down. Disillusionment is a feeling shared by many South Africans. This calls for leaders of stature who will not be swayed by greed – leaders who will act responsibly and with integrity.

For nearly 20 years, our politicians have fed the people with words that reverberate and inspire a sense of hope. Our country needs more than rhetorical brilliance, though – we need leaders who can build a foundation for a politics of empathy and an era of integrity in politics. They should eschew divisiveness, and cultivate a shared consciousness about social justice. In a society marked by inequality, we need leaders with vision and imagination, leaders who will place health care and education at the centre of planning for social change. Leadership matters.

23. The erosion of morality in government

City Press, 28 April 2014

In early 2014, President Jacob Zuma was engulfed in yet another controversy, this time about improper public expenditure on his palatial homestead at Nkandla in KwaZulu-Natal. There were some troubling responses by the ruling party and some of its supporters to the 'Nkandla crisis', and I wrote this piece to explore the parallels between failures of political morality in apartheid and post-apartheid South Africa.

LIVE THEATRE TOUCHES our lives most profoundly when it jolts us out of our comfort zones, revealing our complacency about who we are as individuals and as a society. The 'statement' plays staged by Athol Fugard, John Kani and Winston Ntshona in the apartheid years portrayed the reality of apartheid for black people in all their diversity. Whether it was *Sizwe Banzi Is Dead* or *The Island* in the early 1970s, or *The Blood Knot* in the late 1960s, the goal was always to show on stage what some wanted to push into the realm of the 'invisible'.

The play *A Human Being Died that Night*, which recently completed its run at the Fugard Theatre in Cape Town and the Market Theatre in Johannesburg, probes the dark past of Eugene de Kock as head of the apartheid government's 'covert operations unit' stationed at Vlakplaas. The play, however, is not just about De Kock. Nor is it simply about apartheid-era atrocities. Its power lies in the fact that it reminds us of the moral lapses in the government at that time – and among the voters who kept it in power – that encouraged De Kock, and sanctioned his actions.

Furthermore, the play urges its audience to expand its consciousness and consider that it may be wrong to call De Kock 'prime evil', because he is the product of a time when moral codes were turned upside down, and few seemed to care. We witness on stage the lonely figure of Eugene de Kock, played by Matthew Marsh, cast away by his former bosses in government and by a society of voters who offered tacit support for apartheid's destruction. While De Kock and his men undertook one 'successful' operation after another, receiving accolades that made him the most decorated police officer under apartheid, the electoral tides in support of the apartheid government kept on rising. 'White South Africans were very happy to be protected,' says De Kock's character. 'They didn't care *how*. Or what our *methods* were.'

As brutal as De Kock's actions were, they were part of a larger systemic strategy of the exclusion of black South Africans, denying them the privilege bestowed upon white people by virtue of their whiteness, and very few people cared enough to raise their voices against the corrupt and brutal system of apartheid. Those in positions of political power, who could have done more to reverse the carnage in a country that was headed towards becoming a failed state, chose not to act but to hide behind a wall of denials, refusing to take responsibility for the chaos that was unfolding. A culture of collective blindness prevailed: see no evil, hear no evil, speak no evil.

What about the complicity of the voters, and those who did not necessarily support the apartheid government, yet benefited from white privilege? I have asked myself how conscience can become suppressed to the point where people allow themselves to commit horrible acts against others, or turn a blind eye to those acts. Should one also ask, what kind of society enables such suppression? Does knowing that the actions of the government which one votes for are wrong, and persisting in voting for it, reveal a greater depth of moral decadence than having the blindness, lack of reflexive capacity, or malfunctioning ethical compass that renders one unable even to *realise* that something is terribly wrong?

No question about it, the moral compass of the nation plunged to a new low in the South Africa of the 1980s, marked by the brutal necklace murders by black youths in the townships; the destruction of black life in the townships by young white conscripts and vigilante groups; and the dehumanisation, torture, poisoning and assassination of anti-apartheid activists. When De Kock's character describes the horrific human destruction that he and others committed in the name of the apartheid government and the white society which they served, one is reminded of the levels to which our country plunged. It had to be done to maintain the status quo, De Kock's character tells his interviewer. Nobody cared how. The moral question of whether an action *ought* to be done or whether a decision *ought* to be taken was replaced with one that placed no limits on actions: *Can* it be done? The end justifies the means, a conviction that everything is possible. This was Hannah Arendt's observation in her discussion of totalitarian societies.

It is difficult to watch *A Human Being Died that Night*, and listen to Eugene de Kock's character, without asking oneself how he might have turned out had there been a significant chorus of voices by white South Africans speaking out against apartheid, and refusing to support it through their votes. Today, however, those who supported apartheid – a system declared to be a crime against humanity by the United Nations – and those who benefited from it, are caught up in a vortex of denial and evasion of the reality that they are 'guiltily implicated', to borrow a term from Alexander and Margarite Mitscherlich, in the story of De Kock's past. The tragic part of denials is not only that they render the painful reality of those who suffered under apartheid invisible, but also that they silence the subject's own conscience.

Some may find comfort, no matter how small, in words of acknowledgement such as this statement in the academic journal *Psychoanalytic Dialogues* by Melanie Suchet, a South African psychoanalyst now living in New York: 'I do believe that assuming individual responsibility, as a white South African, for the acts of apartheid committed while I lived under the system, even if not directly committed by me, is a necessary act of collective moral responsibility.' What is at stake is the rising tide of uncomfortable truths about the past, including, on the one hand, the reality of the relegation of black people to the status of third class 'citizens', and on the other, what it meant to be a white person under apartheid. Some readers may protest: 'We are tired of hearing about apartheid'; or, 'Here you go again, blaming white people'. Please bear with me, because I think there are important lessons to be learnt from Eugene de Kock's story.

Moving from live theatre to political theatre, *A Human Being Died that Night* confronts audiences with a reality that goes beyond De Kock: the paradox that the strategies of apartheid's survival may serve as a prototype for how today's government 'engineers' a society of voters that will ensure its continuing or lasting power. A culture of corruption, personal enrichment, control and fear – and a personality cult around President Jacob Zuma – is chipping away at the moral foundation that was established in the early years of our democracy for us to pursue a meaningful vision rather than greed and the power of position. Nelson Mandela's wise leadership is so badly needed at this time, and his words always invite reflection: 'Honour belongs to those who never forsake the truth, even when things seem dark and grim.' Yet the erosion of values and what seems to me to be a lowering of the shame threshold among the leaders of Mandela's party has been relentless, and the tragic social and cultural repercussions of this erosion are now in plain sight. Once again, with the release of the findings about Nkandla, the cast of actors in this shameful saga shows little sign of wishing to reclaim the proud legacy of the party that the majority of South Africans loved and looked up to in order to restore its moral centre.

The moral crisis of 'Nkandla' may seem like a minor transgression compared to the tragic history of our country, the gradual and violent erosion of moral values portrayed so clearly in De Kock's story. But the response to 'Nkandla' is part of an insidious pattern of disregard for the values that restored our pride as a nation in the first few years of our democracy, and a systematic effort to keep Zuma in power. His presidency has fostered a culture of 'unlimited possibilities', to invoke Arendt once more, and this protection of government power at all costs is not new in South Africa. It is not a good story to tell. It is a chilling narrative of self-serving agendas, and seems to have less to do with serving the people than ruling them as subjects. Zuma's response to a question by Hajra Omarjee during an interview on African News Network after his 'State of the Nation' address in Parliament in February 2014 is a striking illustration of this point. Asked by Omarjee to explain why, despite burgeoning service delivery protests, the results of local government elections continued to favour the ANC, Zuma pointed out that critics of the ANC failed to understand that protests against the ANC's lack of delivery did not imply hatred of the ANC. In his view, Zuma explained, the protesters were like children running to a parent 'asking for a new pair of trousers, or asking for sweets'. Setting aside the patronising tone for a moment, it struck me that these are sentiments that would be expressed by a monarch rather than a president of a country.

Others have bestowed this status of 'king' on Zuma. For example, Supra Mahumapelo, ANC chairman in North West, informs us that many people regard Zuma as their king. Accordingly, a king 'must always be respected and embraced by everybody'. As a concrete expression of this sentiment in the immediate aftermath of the release of the Nkandla report, thousands of people came out to show their support for Zuma wearing t-shirts inscribed with the words: 'We stand by our President.'

It does not matter what accusations he faces: Zuma has built a protective wall around himself that renders him immune to any serious consequences for his actions. There is something deeply dehumanising about this, that a man who has faced a string of scandals, past and present, is our president. Are there no men or women of integrity within the ANC who can uphold a higher standard of leadership – a moral leadership – than the ANC has delivered in recent years? 'What's happening in this world, good people? Who cares for who in this world?' Sizwe in the play *Sizwe Banzi is Dead* ponders this question in the face of the indignities he suffers at the hands of his white employer. It is an insult to the dignity of voters when the president compares their protests about poor service delivery to a child's demands for little pleasures. Giving voters t-shirts inscribed with words of support for Zuma, and busing them to central points where they are used as human banners to bolster the president's image, is an insult to their dignity.

Instead of using voters in the same way that the apartheid government used its voters by keeping the truth away from view, or creating a complicated matrix of rationalisations to make the truth invisible, the ANC government's leadership should explain the Public Protector's findings to the voters. They should tell voters that some of the money intended for service delivery programmes was used to build the president's palatial home. Voters should be informed that taxpayers' money was not only used for the president's security and protection, but also for his luxurious comfort.

Instead of surrounding the president with the might of intelligence surveillance, the ANC leadership in government should ask the questions: 'Where are we going: where is all this taking our country?' and 'What should be done?' This is what accountability means.

The collective response of the ANC leadership to the Nkandla report – but also its response to every scandal associated with the president's personal life – is a betrayal of so much of what we believed about the future of our country in the first years of our democracy. It diminishes our human dignity and sense of pride as a nation when our president, as the first citizen, does not seem to appreciate the importance of accountability. Mandela set a beautiful standard when he was president; he served all South Africans, for the greater good of our country. He created a strong sense of social solidarity that united South Africans across racial lines, and made us feel proud to be South Africans. In order to demonstrate the values and principles embodied in the vision that his leadership inspired in the aftermath of apartheid, he honoured court summonses, and duly accepted court decisions. Nelson Mandela was *mindful* in his role of leadership, always focused on the vision of lifting our country out of the chaos we witnessed in the dying days of apartheid, always conscious that his position of leadership was in service of the greater good of society. His mindfulness, in the words of the Chief Justice of the Kenyan Supreme Court, Willy Mutunga, 'made him bigger, not smaller'.

It seems to me that the quest for position and power – to protect the president at all costs – rather than a desire to serve for the greater good of humanity, is what drives the pattern of responses to the various scandals that have been exposed in the media, including the Nkandla affair. And Nobody Cares. It is not surprising that blatant corruption runs rampant in our country. It is a culture that flourishes precisely because of the failure to demonstrate accountability by those in positions of power when they are called to account for their actions, or those of their comrades. We are witnessing the unfolding of the same moral darkness of our past – the same culture of 'unlimited possibilities' that kept the apartheid government in power. To understand how this situation has flourished in our democracy, let us look no further than the man who in our mind has come to represent the 'prime evil' of our historical past. Eugene de Kock now carries not only his own guilt and responsibility for this shameful past, he has become carrier of the shame and guilt of those who chose to silence their conscience, to eschew their moral responsibility.

Voters – 'We stand by our President' – will soon present Zuma with a second term. This strong spirit of support for the president regardless of what he has done was captured in a statement published in the *Sunday Times* in May 2006 by David Masondo, then chairman of the Young Communist League. Zuma, Masondo said, 'has the right to have sex with any consenting adult — to argue that he should not be president because he had sex with an HIV-positive consenting adult is morally wrong'.

What lies on our country's horizon of hope? Dare we hope to overcome the moral crisis that is upon us? I think we can. The voices we have heard from civil society and others across the country; the demonstration of support for the Public Protector by Archbishop Thabo Makgoba, Archbishop Desmond Tutu, and other members of the clergy; the continued vigilance of the media and their dedication to reporting the not-so-good stories from the echelons of power – these are signs of a healthy democracy. Yet what is missing in our democracy is a spirit of human solidarity that transcends the commitment to membership of one's racial group or political party. The intolerance inherent in fighting between political parties – and sometimes killings – during election campaigns reflects this lack of human solidarity, a lack of compassion for others, and not being able to extend care to them as members of the human community. The ANC leadership's public display of intolerance of criticism, through their words and actions, closes the social space for dialogue and debate, and stifles our growth as a country into greatness.

SEEDS OF
DISCONTENT

*'If the greater challenge of economic transformation
is not met, what has already been achieved in South
Africa could be lost, and something worse could
happen. The next revolution might not necessarily
be a racial one, but one in which the masses rise
against the new breed of beneficiaries of privilege.'*

24. Counting the costs of a nation in the making

Sunday Times, 27 August 2006

I wrote this article in response to a discussion document on macroso-cial trends in South Africa, released by the Presidency under Thabo Mbeki. Entitled A Nation in the Making, *the report surveyed the material circumstances of South Africans, revealing disheartening facts about family relationships and structures.*[20]

ON ANY GIVEN day, thousands of commuters from Cape Town's townships and informal settlements navigate their way to the city and its suburbs to go to work, shop, take their children to school, or look for work. They pack the crowded third-class train carriages and hazardous minibus taxis to capacity, often travelling in speeding trains with open doors, and in taxis that are unroadworthy. The commuters have no power to change the status of their transport; most of them are driven by the quest for the dignity of earning a living and providing for their families.

Many of these people exemplify the migration trends described in a report released by the Presidency at the end of June. Bearing a future-oriented title, *A Nation in the Making*, the document examines the macrosocial trends in our post-apartheid democracy.

One of the greatest challenges the country has faced since 1994 is the movement of large sections of the population towards urban areas, and the multitude of problems resulting from overcrowd-ing, the rapid growth of informal settlements, unemployment,

---

[20]   The Presidency, *A Nation in the Making – A discussion document on macro-social trends in South Africa*, http://www.thepresidency.gov.za/pebble. asp?relid=348.

and rising crime and mortality rates. The report tries to elucidate macrosocial changes in migration, and provides some data on the implications for households and families. According to the report, about 75% of all migration is to urban areas, with the following provincial pattern: Gauteng, 32.8%, Western Cape, 14.8%, and KwaZulu-Natal, 14.1%. The Eastern Cape and Limpopo suffer the biggest losses of people, as the movement is greater towards those regions – in these instances, the Western Cape and Gauteng – that promise more opportunities for employment.

Included in the report is a discussion of 'unnatural' causes of mortality. Statistics on HIV and AIDS-related deaths are provided. The report concludes that HIV is 'a pandemic under silent attack, [and] its fatal impact is starting to express itself palpably in both morbidity and mortality'. Perhaps the most troubling conclusion is one that we all know so well: that those who are most affected are young, able-bodied adults 'who would most likely be parents of young children and possibly breadwinners ...'

The picture is a grim one for our 'nation in the making' when one considers the implications of some of the report's findings for family life. In this respect, I was struck by three observations. The first is the 'poverty trap' that threatens households headed by women with few or no skills to draw on. For rural women who are trapped in the 'second economy', whose mothers experienced the disruption of family life and the humiliation of the migrant labour system, this is history repeating itself. The second observation concerns the disintegration of family life caused not only by migration, but also by AIDS-related mortality.

The third troubling finding concerns the impact of macrosocial trends on the structure of the family and on parenting. Some shifts are painfully obvious: children whose parents die of AIDS are brought up by older siblings, aging grandparents, or neighbours;

the disappearance of child care as parents are forced to leave their children with neighbours or older children while they try to survive in a new urban setting. Other shifts are perhaps less easily quantifiable, but equally profound: the stress of caring for a family member who is HIV-positive and/or suffering from an AIDS-related disease; the psychological impact of crime and violence. Some of the changes in the macrosocial sphere discussed in the report have had major impacts, especially on black families. Some have had irreversible consequences, and continue to put younger members of black communities at risk.

The family is a microcosm of many interrelated systems, and the notion of 'family' evokes feelings of safety, security and belonging. Families play an important role in the socialisation of young people, who are the future of this nation in the making. Stability within families and within communities ensures that young people develop into responsible adults who can reflect on their actions and make reasoned decisions for the public good as citizens in a democratic society.

Crime statistics presented in the report point to a staggering increase in young offenders. This is not at all surprising, given the family disintegration portrayed in the report. This may be the reason why the report calls for the strengthening of household stability and families to provide a nurturing environment for children.

As a young psychologist during the apartheid years, I often worked with young black men who were full of rage. I still see that rage in some young black men today. They wake up every morning to a yawning void. Their lives count for nothing. They look around them and see poverty, and they feel humiliated. It is an economic poverty, but also a poverty of dignity passed on from the generation before them.

We must begin to think creatively about ways of helping them to reclaim their dignity and to reverse the destructive effects of the macrosocial trends that have been part of this nation in the making. If we don't find some way to repay the debt owed to the casualties of change in our society, their anger will blow up long before Jacob Zuma's rallying song, 'Leth'uMshini Wami' (bring my machine gun), inspires them to do just that.

25. Crisis calls for leaders with moral courage

CAPE TIMES, 13 JUNE 2008

> *The wave of xenophobia in 2008 in which foreign Africans were driven from South African townships were a dismaying reminder of the political violence of the 1970s and 1980s. Had South Africans forgotten what it was like to be victims of oppression? In this article, I sought to identify the roots of the violence, and argued that we needed strong political leadership which could restore people's faith in our new democracy and its ability to improve their economic circumstances.*

COULD SOMETHING LIKE the violence of the 1970s and 1980s happen again? Last week, this question dominated conversations in Langa, where I joined members of my extended family and others who had come from communities in surrounding townships to evening prayer meetings held to mourn the death of my aunt. After arriving in Cape Town with a nursing diploma in the 1950s, my aunt had lived in Kensington, District Six, Langa, Gugulethu, Nyanga, Khayelitsha, and Langa once again, where she had bought a house and lived until her ill health and death.

Given the xenophobic violence that has erupted around Cape Town and across the country, the question seems an obvious one for people who, like my aunt, have experienced at first hand the violent brutality of forced removals and the Group Areas Act, the turmoil of political violence, and with it the destruction of their homes. Whether it was the brutal violence of the South African Defence Force (SADF) which invaded the black townships in the 1980s; the murderous rampages of the 'witdoeke', the black collaborators who did the SADF's bidding in Cape Town townships; or the 'necklace' murders by ruthless gangs who aligned themselves with the liberation struggle, for many of the people who came to mourn my aunt's death, the viciousness of the violence visited upon their lives and their communities may be in the past, but that past remains etched in their collective memory.

'When I think about these poor people they are chasing away from their homes,' an older woman says, referring to the African immigrants who have been displaced, 'my heart bleeds, because I know the feeling of losing everything you have worked hard for – the terror and utter helplessness, not knowing where to start and where to go.' We are sitting around a paraffin heater as she continues to recount her experiences in Nyanga more than 20 years ago, when her home was burnt down by the 'witdoeke' and her husband shot dead by SADF soldiers.

At some point in the retelling of her story, she stops in mid-sentence and looks down at the cup of tea in her hand, with tears welling in her eyes. Another woman in the circle shakes her head, wiping the tears streaking her cheeks with the back of her hand. There is a moment of reflective silence among all of us sitting in the warm corner of the room with cups in our hands.

During prayers earlier that evening, the cleric from St Columbus Church in Gugulethu who had delivered the funeral sermon asked: What will the violence accomplish? What has happened to *ubuntu*, the basic human compassion that binds us as brothers and sisters, the children of one God? Various nods of agreement came from around the small living room. There was no doubt in my mind that everyone reflected on the violence against African immigrants with deep condemnation.

There are echoes from the past in the violence witnessed in areas surrounding our beloved city. But while these events have evoked shame and outrage among many of us, this is also an occasion of which we South Africans can be proud. For, unlike in the past, when the country was divided by fear and hatred, with only a scattered few publicly condemning in words and in actions the massive displacement of people who were forced to be second-class citizens in their own country – both as a result of oppressive laws and of political violence – today we stand united, coloured, white, black, rich and poor, against the inhumanity visited upon fellow human beings.

We are full of praise for all those who refused to submit to fear and silence in the past. This newspaper should be proud to count its own among those who defied the prevailing political tide of the past. I am reminded of Tony Weaver and Chris Bateman who insisted on giving readers a more accurate picture of the violence perpetrated by state security organs, which the government was trying to conceal. Many Capetonians courageously stepped up when they saw the suffering of others, some quietly and others more visibly; among many whose names come to mind, Reverend John Freeth stood in front of SADF trucks in Nyanga when they were wreaking murderous rampage, and tried to care for some of the dying people left in their trail. Thousands of residents in some of the townships in the Cape Town region were displaced, or left homeless. These South Africans and many others who were moved by the bond of common humanity led us to a better place, to this moment we can build on as a society, united against the horrors committed against fellow human beings today.

There's no doubt that there is an element of thuggery in the mindless violence we have seen in recent weeks. But a large part of it has to do with the effects of unfulfilled promises, a life of deep poverty and deprivation which has not changed – and in many cases worsened – since the dawn of liberation 14 years ago. People who feel the pinch of poverty and unemployment feel that democ-

119

racy has failed them. The issue of economic justice in South Africa cries out for resolution.

In earlier reports of xenophobic violence, Somalis were the main targets of attacks. Somalis moved into local areas and set up their shops from the small profits they had made from their street stalls. They brought to the country very astute entrepreneurial skills, which, for a range of reasons, are evidently lacking among local people. One has to consider that the group of Somalis who ventured out into the world seeking to build a better life may have had a particular edge that enabled them to develop in the way that they have within local communities.

Local people watched these immigrants who had been in the country for only a few years rise and excel in small businesses in ways that they and the generation before them had never been able to achieve. The Somalis worked hard at developing their shops, becoming employers of local people. They lived a better quality of life, one which local people had given up hoping for. It was a powder keg waiting to explode.

And so the struggle must continue for people to have a better life, and for their voices to be heard. Sadly, this time the violent struggle was against their African brothers and sisters. They are, after all, the 'enemy within' – it seems when the pie is just the tiniest sliver, your own sister becomes your enemy in the fight for survival.

My heart aches for all of our ravaged and ravaging people. Sometimes I feel I am wailing like a mourner for the crushed hopes and desecrated dreams of just 14 years ago. Economic injustice is indeed at the bowels of the problem in our country. Unless and until we regulate our huge corporate behemoth and start the process of the redistribution of economic opportunity in all its forms – education, training, apprenticeship, and a different kind of black economic empowerment that will be aimed at the poorest – we are doomed.

My view, I must say, is that there is a crisis of leadership in many of our institutions, not just in government. As for the government, with the squabbles we have witnessed through the media both within the ANC and among political parties, some drastic shifts need to occur in order to put the country back on its feet, restoring the pride and sense of hope that inspired us to be excited about Thabo Mbeki when he was inaugurated as the second president of a truly democratic South Africa. Right now, he and many other ANC leaders have become a defensive bastion for the corruption and preoccupation with the accumulation of wealth among some in positions of leadership in government. (I'm afraid that is true of Jacob Zuma as well, who, in spite of facing serious corruption charges, aspires to become our next president.) Sadly, this paves the way for demagogues. They will be inspired more by personal ambition and material wealth than a desire to lead South Africa and its people with the vision and courage that brought us through difficult challenges, and to memorable historic moments since the release of Nelson Mandela in 1990.

What could be more obvious than the idea that what is needed in South Africa is a massive public works programme – even if it means the dismissal and actual prosecution of corrupt politicians, and fewer submarines, airplanes and bribes?

We need to establish a sense of dignity for the young people surrounded by poverty and depravity, before their anger blows up. It seems to me that we've had a small taste of that anger in the xenophobic violence we have seen around the country.

Last Saturday I was doing volunteer work in one of the shelters for displaced immigrants as part of the Trauma Centre's mental health support. During a conversation with a woman from the Congo, a group of children gathered around us and wanted our attention. One of the girls, a tiny seven-year-old, quietly and elegantly climbed on the table and sat there with her arms folded while others started telling me about their experiences: how they had lost their books, pens and uniforms, and how they wished they could return to school. One girl told me how the coloured children in her school demanded her school money, telling her 'jou ma se ...' when she refused, and that her homework book was 'in the fire lighted by the Xhosas in my home'. The beautiful girl with big round eyes on the table waited her turn, and with a soft voice said: 'My dog did not burn in the fire. She has three puppies. But we left them there. My other dog I left in the Congo.'

This little girl and the many other vulnerable children, including those born into poverty in South Africa, deserve a chance in life. They need a chance to break the cycle of trauma so that they can live meaningful lives, and one day, when they sit around the fire and reflect on the past, their stories should not be stories of lives of long suffering, of violence and more displacement, but stories of lives filled with purpose. For that to happen, we need leaders who can lead with clarity, meaningful vision, and moral courage in this time of crisis in our country.

26. The dream that can no longer be deferred

Mail & Guardian, August 2011

At a time when Julius Malema – then still leader of the ANC Youth League – was repeatedly in the news, I attended a performance of Rewind: A Cantata for Voice, Tape and Testimony *by Philip Miller, which provided a powerful counterpoint to Malema's message of discontent, and pointed to an alternative way of dealing with the legacy of the past and its potential to explode in the present.*

WHAT HAPPENS WHEN we avoid facing the past? Does it haunt us, yielding feelings of shame, guilt or anger? Or do we deny it and the feelings it evokes, and then pursue a quest to 'move on' and forget? Does the past play itself out symbolically in our lives, transforming us into victims, heroes or villains? Does it transform into a language of hate and destructive engagement in the public sphere? Or does it explode into violence, whether real or symbolic, against an 'Other'?

These are not just rhetorical questions; they are questions of profound significance in a society like ours whose history is steeped in repression and violence. They are necessary because they have implications for our understanding of how 'the past' may play itself out in repetition in times of crisis in our society. Past injustices are often collectively remembered by groups that have suffered oppression and gross human rights violations at certain critical times of the group's social life. These collective memories of past traumas may be violently acted out when the level of frustration proliferates and escalates.

The parallels between the rising discontent we have witnessed among the majority of South Africans who are still waiting for meaningful transformation in their lives, almost 20 years since liberation from apartheid rule, and the frustration observed among African Americans a century after their liberation from slavery, calls to mind the words of the African-American poet Langston Hughes. Hughes wrote his poem 'Harlem' in the early 1950s as a warning to America about the powder keg of frustration among black Americans. When the dreams, hopes and aspirations of a people are 'deferred' or frustrated, he wrote, they will 'explode'. The African-American civil rights movement some years later could be seen as the 'explosion' that Hughes had predicted in his poem a decade earlier.

I have been concerned about the potential for 'explosion' in our society for a few years now. It has reappeared, brought into focus by Julius Malema's words and actions in recent months, especially his speech at the ANC Youth League Conference in June. A central feature of the Youth League leader's 'sophisticated terrain of struggle' – as he referred to his call for economic freedom – is the past, and the urgent need to redress it. Malema places himself at centre of this narrative about the past, and connects his own individual memory of the past with the collective historical experience of the people on whose behalf he speaks: 'We are children of domestic workers,' he said, 'we know what it means not to find a plate of food on the table.'

This was not simply an interesting detail about his past family life, but rather, more fundamentally, a persuasive public testimony about a world in which helpless parents worried how they were going to feed their children. The current reality of Malema's supporters is inextricably bound up with their past, a past that Malema shares. Therefore, despite his lifestyle, he can rely on the powerful bond with his supporters because of a shared past he is able to articulate on their behalf.

The memory of long-past traumatic injustices cannot be silenced. Yet some have called for a 'forgetting' of the past. They argue that 'digging up' the past is a senseless exercise that turns back the wheel of history, perpetuates victimhood, and undermines a future-oriented political vision. It is true that the emergence of collective memory of victimhood into public discourse may re-ignite hatred of historical enemies. For people who want to forget the past, however, 'remembering' threatens their deepest sense of humanity because of the memory of what they did or did not do, of their complicity or their silence. In contrast, Malema articulates, in powerful language and imagery, the sense of growing frustration among people for whom nothing has changed, because they have not tasted the fruits that political transformation promised.

Making the beneficiaries of apartheid privilege 'return' what they acquired during the apartheid era is the only chance of restoring the unfulfilled hopes of the oppressed, and the only way to deal effectively with the discontent and demands for real transformation. At the same time, however, Malema is advocating a model of remembering that flirts with the most destructive aspects of memory: revenge. With time, continuing the trend he has started is bound to ferment into anger, confrontation and revenge.

This is why South Africans need an alternative way of remembering the past. We need a new public discourse that is imbued with moral possibilities and a sense of responsible citizenship – to face the past in order to gain perspective about the present, including a capacity for understanding the experiences that confront many young people whose lives have not been touched by the waves of economic opportunity that have been rolled out in the name of black economic empowerment.

One has to be mindful of the dilemmas inherent in the 'project' of facing the past. As Martha Minow, dean of law at

Harvard University, puts it in considering the question of facing the past, there may be 'too much memory or not enough; too much enshrinement of victimhood or insufficient memorialising of victims and survivors; too much past or too little acknowledgement of the past's staging of the present'. The reality of facing historical injustices is that it is not always easy to confront the past, because facing it may uncover difficult truths. Yet avoidance of the past is no longer an option for us South Africans.

We can draw lessons from the memory of the Holocaust and the remembrance of its victims across the globe. The unspeakable crimes of the Holocaust are known not only for their origin in the public statements of the Nazi leader that dazzled the youth of those days, but also for the moral failures of societies of bystanders throughout Nazi Europe who supported Nazi policies. The same can be said about the events that led to the genocide in Rwanda. In all the histories of policies of systematic abuse of marginalised and oppressed groups, there is a society of voters who supported these policies.

The former supporters of oppressive governments are usually the targets of hatred and resentment when the extraordinary hopes of oppressed groups remain unfulfilled. Therefore, the quest for dialogue about the past is a quest to convey the aspiration of preventing discourse driven by hate and build an alternative legacy of a nation in conversation about the past in order to build responsible communities and a more humane future.

I have mentioned that, for a range of factors, facing the past does not come easily. Music and the arts, however, can give shape to our historical legacies, and help us find a language with which to face our history in an attitude of building bridges for human connection across diversity instead of breaking them down. Philip Miller's musical composition *Rewind: A Cantata for Voice, Tape and Testimony* offers an important alternative for engaging with the past. *Rewind* is based on recordings of testimonies of victims and survivors who appeared before the Truth and Reconciliation Commission (TRC). In Miller's musical, we encounter the interweaving of stories of victims, perpetrators and bystanders, all voices from the past, telling the story of the different roles they played.

One of the stories in Miller's performance is based on the testimony of Nomonde Calata, the widow of Fort Calata, one of the 'Cradock Four' executed by apartheid security police. At the TRC hearing, she tried to tell the story of the important role her husband had played as a teacher and community leader who worked hard for the rights and dignity of black people. Her voice, replayed in Miller' musical production, carried all the emotions she experienced when she found out about the vicious murder of her husband.

At one point during her testimony, which was replayed at the staging of *Rewind* at the Baxter Theatre in May, her voice faltered, and then she let out a piercing cry that shattered the stillness of the theatre. It is this wailing voice that Miller resurrects from the archives of TRC narratives. A soloist, Nozuko Teto, then picks up Nomonde Calata's crying voice and represents it through her magnificent and electrifying soprano voice. Several other voices in the choir, with different levels of intensity, male and female voices, sing this wailing cry. The effect is a seamless repetition of this voice-cry that reverberates like a re-enactment of a wound that refuses to be silenced.

Miller seems to be telling the audience: This is not yet past. Indeed, at the end of Miller's show at the Baxter, there is a still and dead silence in the hall after the curtain call. The audience, clearly moved by Miller's unsettling stories, leaves the hall in reflective mood. And here is the power of the creative arts in bringing us to remembering the past: people did not leave after the performance of *Rewind*. Instead, they gathered around each other, and even around strangers, crying, talking to one another, and sharing the most tragic, shameful or confusing aspects of our past.

Through these brief dialogue encounters with one another, we each can take some first steps into the light of hopefulness – hope, not as an abstract concept, but as a moment imbued with the real possibility of deepening a sense of acknowledgement, understanding and respect for one another's pasts. We can begin to feel some wisps of a fresh breeze coming, and be part of that possibility of living reconciliation.

The government should begin to think more creatively about what it can do to offer substantive alternatives to thousands of young black South Africans who wake up every day to face emptiness in their lives. Many of them are living their parents' and grandparents' lives in repetition, and in some cases their lives are worse than those of their parents. The picture is a grim one for many of our young people, and the model that Malema offers – to take back what white people unjustly acquired in the past – inspires them to keep hope alive. Needless to say, for pragmatic (and moral) reasons, it is a model that is bound to fail, and would lead our country to chaos.

Past injustices, and the struggle against these injustices, have led to disruptive consequences across generations of black families. At the same time, generations of many white families have done relatively well and prospered because of the protection, privileges and benefits whites received under apartheid. The heritage of economic oppression and a life of servitude in previous generations continue to put younger members of many black communities in all their diversity at risk. The long and impenetrable shadow of injustice still covers our society, to paraphrase the African-American activist Randall Robinson, and it is a legacy that the post-apartheid government has perpetuated over the past 17 years.

Malema's voice is important for us because, driven by both personal and collective goals, he reminds us of the real possibility for an explosive eruption. This is why I believe it is important that new or alternative conversations emerge at the level of civil society. An honest look at our past would be a good place to start.

RACE, RACISM AND AFFIRMATIVE ACTION

'Clearly, our institutions in South Africa face some challenges in their implementation of equity policies. Yet there are pressing reasons why the quest for equity in our previously divided and unequal society is a moral virtue that we must pursue.'

27. America's silence about the past

Los Angeles Times, 12 July 1999

During my time as a Fellow at Harvard University, I observed that, in many parts of America, a long history of slavery and inequality is shrouded in silence. At the same time, black skin continues to be chained to a burden of proof. In this article I reflected on the lessons Americans could learn from South Africa about the healing power of naming and acknowledging racism.

THERE IS A thread that connects the experiences of all black people everywhere: the burden of skin colour. This fact was brought home to me twice during the past few days, and the fault lines in American race relations were twice exposed.

A discussion about South Africa's Truth and Reconciliation Commission (TRC) always evokes some of the deep currents that run through the American historical memory. But sometimes there is an attempt to redefine, harness, or – worse still – silence these deep-running currents.

This silence was ruptured recently in a sermon by Anthony Miller, assistant priest of Saint Peter's Episcopal Church in Cambridge, Massachusetts. He gave the silence a name, drawing out the historical threads that connect the lives of black people in America and South Africa. He asked: what is the example of South Africa's TRC calling us to do? And: what work needs to be done in respect of unhealed wounds in American society?

Miller posed the most commonly asked questions in every discussion about the TRC that I have led or attended. Taking us down the rigors of personal and historical memory, he mapped the contours that mark the landscape of black life in America, reminded everyone that there is need for truth in our lives, and uttered that most silenced word in American conversations: slavery. His story resonated with mine as a child and adult in apartheid South Africa, marking the first point of connection that linked my past to the historical burden of being black in America.

The story of my life was re-enacted recently when I was looking for a place to rent in the Belmont suburb of Boston. The real estate agents were enthusiastic, saying the right things to dispel the racial attitude that was silently seeping through the conversations with would-be landlords. In an attempt to compensate for my black-ness, the realtors mentioned my 'background' – visiting fellow at Harvard University, clinical psychologist from South Africa – more times than I do in my résumé. But it made no difference that I had the respect of my colleagues in one of Harvard's research institutes.

To many of my prospective landlords, I was merely a black, and that is the only 'credential' that mattered. It occurred to me that white people never have to wonder about the intrusion of race into the important decisions about where they live or work, or where their children go to school. Some of the white people I talked to about my experiences tried to dismiss my suspicions, claiming that race could not have been a factor in the rejections. And when a white friend found out that an apartment I was told had already been rented was still available, they were dumbfounded, a response that says more about their discomfort about the subject of racism than any other feelings they might have had about my experiences.

Why should the subject of racism bring shame and embar-rassment to some whites even if they are not the ones expressing those attitudes? The answer lies in the complex and intricate past that is part of the historical memory of societies that have to deal with racism. The constant silencing and denial of that memory is an attempt to master, conquer, and finally crush history. It is a history that links them to the evil roots that gave birth to it.

To embrace this history would be to threaten their sense of humanity. So it is better denied as something of the past. When it comes to the question of racism, very few people can confront it openly and truthfully.

But there is indeed a need for truth in our lives. The model of the TRC may not be the answer to the American experience. Yet it offers something of value. The problems of South Africa were addressed – certainly not resolved – through the voices of first-generation victims and perpetrators. The TRC put a face and a name to atrocities of the past. Perpetrators were publicly exposed and rigorously questioned by victims and survivors – a crucial part of healing.

Is there a lesson in this for how to heal the wounds in American society? Its troubling past is removed from the present by several generations. But its legacy continues to live in the silence. When Miller or others ask the question of what needs to be done about unhealed wounds in American society, it is a crying out for the silence to be given a voice.

Facing history can be liberating or imprisoning, says the Pulitzer Prize winner David Shipler. It can unite or divide. South Africa took the risk of facing its history, and there is some satisfaction in knowing that we found a language in which to speak about the ghosts of the past. Even if the burden of being black follows me to foreign lands, even as my life under the scourge of apartheid racism is re-enacted in American society, it gives me a sense of peace to know that, back home, we have figured out a way to talk about the past.

28. The subtleties of bigotry

ThisDay, 15 October 2004

In October 2004, President Thabo Mbeki launched a scathing attack on journalists and others who had questioned the integrity of crime statistics released by the South African Police Service, arguing that their views reflected a racist conception of African men as 'violent sexual predators'.[21] His attack provoked a new debate about racism in South Africa. I was concerned about the direction in which the public conversation had moved; it seemed to reflect a lack of recognition of past patterns of racism, and how racial inequality continued to structure our everyday lives.

THE FACT THAT racism was once pervasive throughout South African society has been all but missing from reactions to President Thabo Mbeki's criticism of statements in the media about rape and other crime statistics. A distant observer might mistakenly believe that the debate over racism is a presidential obsession, and only occurs in the form of altercations in the halls of power between Mbeki and the leader of the Democratic Alliance, Tony Leon.

The issue of racism is far from being a thing of the past; it raises its ugly head in different places, not least among the custodians of the highest values and principles of our society, as borne out by complaints made by Western Cape Judge President John Hlophe. The racism debate, does, however, need to be taken to a higher level, one that will move beyond simple considerations of the legitimacy of Mbeki's judgment that statements about crime in South Africa are motivated by race, or Hlophe's assertion that his white colleagues are racists.

---

[21] IOLnews, 'Mbeki blasts crime stats critics', 1 October 2004, http://www.iol.co.za/news/south-africa/mbeki-blasts-crime-stats-critics-1.223129#.UxAlRIWj0ns

Searching for evidence of racism in statements that are unpleasant and difficult to accept, or in racially ambiguous behaviour, would be fruitless. If such statements and behaviours are indeed motivated by racism, those responsible usually deny it, and they are quite skilled at presenting plausible and perfectly acceptable explanations to show why their remarks and behaviours are not racist. In the end, those making the 'racism' judgment are accused of 'misinterpreting' what was intended. They are therefore left with the burden of feeling either angry or foolish, since it is hard to prove something that is not obvious, and easy to deny it because it is difficult to pinpoint. A denial of racist motives turns an accusation of racism on its head, making the accusers feel inadequate and powerless.

One question that will raise the public debate on racism is: what can be done about it? A starting point would be to acknowledge, instead of deny, that ten years of a change of laws will not result in an automatic change of attitudes, and that racism will continue to seep – in subtle and not-so-subtle ways – into our new democracy.

As we think about how to move this debate forward, we should focus on the psychological legacy of apartheid racism – the experiences of white privilege while other racial groups were excluded from economic, educational, and occupational opportunities, which instilled a sense of superiority in the minds of many of our white compatriots. We should also not lose sight of the long-term effects of a system that strategically instilled inferiority by closing the doors of opportunity to blacks.

The legacy of apartheid lies both in what is visible and what is invisible. Under apartheid, it was not only legal but also socially acceptable for whites to treat members of other racial groups as inferior. Ten years ago, there was a shift in the political landscape, and the laws changed. Racist behaviour was no longer appropriate.

South Africans, however, did not become colour-blind, and attitudes did not change overnight. Thus, expecting all white people to behave towards black people without being influenced by their racial advantage under apartheid – consciously or otherwise – may be unrealistic. Old attitudes and assumptions continue to influence behaviour at an implicit level.

Given the introduction of new laws, whites who are caught up in some of the old stereotypical attitudes are under pressure to disguise these subtle tendencies in their behaviour when they are pointed out to them. And this is the greatest challenge. The brand of racism witnessed in workplaces and in everyday social interaction today is less virulent than the one that was legalised under apartheid; it 'sneaks' in without conscious awareness.

I have had numerous conversations with friends and colleagues about their work experiences, even in the most liberal South African institutions. A black colleague who was recently appointed to a senior position in a previously white academic institution related an experience of what he perceived as an example of attempts to undermine his academic achievements. One of his white colleagues came to his office to congratulate him on the recognition he had received from international scholars. As he was leaving, however, the white colleague remarked: 'I wonder what will happen when the bubble bursts.'

The outright racism of the past may be absent, but its deep-seated influence is palpable. Some whites feel diminished by black colleagues who are productive and competent. It is hard to change the world view they were brought up with, which taught them that blacks are inferior. In their minds, as 'affirmative action appointees', blacks are only there to reflect diversity, not to be proficient in the new roles that have become available to them. They are more comfortable with blacks as underachievers to be 'helped' along.

When they are presented with proof to the contrary, this brings out their worst insecurities. They try to deny the evidence before them through various behaviours and statements such as the 'bubble' story cited above. The tragedy is that white people often don't 'hear' themselves when they engage in behaviour that negates the performance of colleagues from other racial groups. There is a discreet silence about race in some circles, especially in liberal academic institutions, precisely because racism is such a sensitive issue, and difficult to discuss. Surprisingly, even at the highest levels of leadership in the country, our leaders have simply engaged in the polemics of race. Very rarely have they inspired creative solutions to the problem of racism.

Racism is an enduring problem in societies with a history of legalised discrimination. WEB du Bois, the scholar and American civil rights fighter, predicted that 'the problem of the 20th century will be the problem of the colour line'. Well, we are in the 21st century now, and racism comes to us not in the blatant prejudice of the previous century, but in very subtle forms. Doors have been opened for people of other races to places previously reserved for whites, but many black people continue to feel like unwelcome guests in their workplaces. Some whites can't shake off their mistrust of blacks, which runs in the very fibre of their being; in their minds lurks the belief that blacks 'can't handle' this or that.

Many institutions that say all the right things about transformation and diversity are unwilling to recognise this type of racism. This blindness will be overcome only if we start to think deeply, seriously, and rigorously about the subtleties of bigotry that continue to plague our young democracy.

29. Onwards (or backwards) into the 21st century

Monday Paper, University of Cape Town, 7 May 2007

In his inaugural lecture at the University of Cape Town in April 2007, Professor David Benatar argued against the adoption of policies of affirmative action. His lecture, entitled 'Justice, Diversity and Affirmative Action', sparked off a major debate in the media as well as university forums, including a campus debate with Professor Martin Hall, at the time vice-chancellor of transformation. The way in which the debate was arranged and conducted inspired me to contribute the following article to the ongoing discussion about race-based policy and transformation at UCT.[22]

INAUGURAL LECTURES ARE opportunities for colleagues who have achieved full academic rank to showcase their work and to 'launch' their ideas and scholarly pursuits in the presence of peers and other members of the university community. These lectures usually have a freshness that offers new insights. They inspire, set the tone, and offer leadership to those who will follow, both students and fellow members of the academic community.

Professor David Benatar's inaugural lecture last week broke with this tradition by discussing themes, concepts and arguments that are well-established in debates on affirmative action, at least since the 1980s. All are in agreement about the timeliness of Benatar's application of the globally familiar anti-affirmative action

---

[22] A shortened version of Professor Benatar's lecture appeared in the *Cape Times* on 12 April 2007. For the text of this article, and exchanges between Professors Benatar and Hall, see *Monday Paper*, Vol. 26 no. 5, 23 April 2007, http://www.uct.ac.za/mondaypaper/archives/?paper=254. For Professor Benatar's response to this article, see *Monday Paper*, Vol. 26 no. 7, 21 May 2007, http://www.uct.ac.za/mondaypaper/archives/?id=6344.

arguments to the concerns that some have about equity policies at UCT. Benatar opened a window through which we can look to see how far we have come in our transformation policies, and where we are headed.

The invitation by Professor Martin Hall to debate the issues Professor Benatar had raised in his inaugural lecture was an important opportunity for us, as staff and students, to enter into an honest debate and to hear views from opposite ends of the debate on the university's equity policies. Sadly, this opportunity was lost when Professor Benatar unilaterally decided to change the terms of engagement agreed on between himself, Professor Hall and me as chair of the debate on Monday 16 April.

What astonished me was not simply that Professor Benatar had decided to change the rules of engagement, but that he considered it conceivable that he could proceed on his own terms. A basic principle was violated: the maintenance of a respectful level of decorum in a debate between colleagues.

The gist of the question and answer format of Professor Benatar's 'debate' with Professor Hall had to do with his interpretation of the university's appointment policies as race-based, and his insistence that racial preference is tantamount to making appointment 'on grounds of biology and not ability'. Most of what Professor Benatar called the 'to and fro' of debate as a way of 'getting to the truth' was a carefully crafted line of questioning – at times conducted like an interrogation – which attempted to force Professor Hall into accepting the 'biology or ability' thesis.

I was troubled by Professor Benatar's narrow focus on singling out race when the university's policy, clarified repeatedly by Professor Hall, plainly recognises the pivotal role of academic merit and professional excellence for staff appointments. Professor Benatar seems more concerned about the racial transformation of staff appointments at UCT than about the shifts in the gender landscape at UCT. The question is, why?

The university's employment equity policies also consider merit along with gender and disability as grounds for preference. The 'biology' of gender, and the fact that there are more white women in positions of leadership than there were when he was a student at UCT, have not raised his ire. Nowhere in his argument does Professor Benatar complain that a white female employee, who may be preferred on the grounds of the university's equity policies, may be hired 'on the grounds of biology and not ability'. Surprisingly, his 'weighting of race affects quality' argument does not seem to apply to an approach that would favour a heavy weighting of class, which he is advocating.

There are fault lines in Professor Benatar's anti-affirmative action language. Focusing on class instead of race in the South African context may, in the end, be a distinction without difference for the majority of the poor, who are black people in all their diversity. This is particularly true in the Western Cape. UCT's policies ought to consider how best to create opportunities for the many young people whose world of disadvantage may close the door of opportunity, and lock them into perpetual cycles of exclusion. We cannot be blind to the racial inequities that continue to exist in our country. Our policies of fairness and equity at UCT must address the problems of economic need; they must also continue to address the issues of gender and race.

This debate on the university's equity policies is happening at all levels of our existence – as students and staff, white and black, male and female. Some of the debates are part of the larger context of our search for identity in a changing society, and they touch our deepest and most hidden fears about what it means to be white at UCT, and what it means to be black. These issues require a much more thoughtful debate, and mutually respectful dialogue. The test of our progress will be measured by our ability to learn to talk to one another, and to listen attentively to others who may be different from us.

UCT is not the same university it was 25 years ago. Change may be happening too fast for some, and too slow for others. And yet, many may feel that nothing has changed at UCT. These feelings and perceptions may be at the heart of our deepest, unnamed fears. No single discipline can provide answers to the challenges we face as an institution. Diversity has never been more important than it is now. We all must draw on our different perspectives, bring our best collective thinking, and consider the new opportunities for dialogue that Monday's debate at UCT created.

Professor Benatar's inaugural lecture has raised a subject that affects all of us at UCT. Our commitment to critical analysis, to challenging and questioning the university's policies, is part of our right to freedom of speech. Academic freedom also means speaking responsibly, listening appreciatively, and conducting ourselves in public debates with one another with the integrity that a world-class university requires. By engaging in public debate about difficult questions that affect our institution, we are responding to a call to become role models of all colours and levels of advantage or disadvantage, and to lead with grace and elegance in the name of this institution that has such a great vision for transformation.

30. Affirmative action: We need nuanced debate

Cape Times, 7 May 2007

I felt the issue of the transformation of historically white institutions resonated beyond the halls of the academy. I wrote this to extend the debate to a wider audience.

IT IS A SHAME that Professor David Benatar ('Affirmative action supporters are still getting it wrong', *Cape Times*, 3 May) has resorted to derogatory references to his colleagues who disagree with him instead of guiding readers into the deepening of intellectual debate on the issue of affirmative action.

It was interesting that a letter written by one of his supporters, MG Warburg ('Benatar's view stands', *Cape Times*, 4 May) mentions Thomas Sowell's study on the failure of affirmative action. There is a remarkable similarity between Benatar's central arguments and those in Sowell's book. These include Sowell's view that black role models are not an essential part of the education of blacks; that affirmative action has disproportionately benefited blacks from affluent backgrounds, or blacks who are no longer disadvantaged; and that the circumstances of blacks born and brought up in disadvantage are irredeemable.

Sowell's empirical research on the effects of affirmative action in India, Sri Lanka, Malaysia, Nigeria and the United States has been hailed by some as an extraordinary study. Others in the scholarly community have criticised his work as reflecting the conservative views associated with Stanford University's Hoover Institute to which Sowell is affiliated. One can understand these critiques because the Hoover Institute's past and present fellows include some of the most influential leaders in conservative politics in history, such as Ronald Reagan, Margaret Thatcher and Condoleezza Rice.

The problem with MG Warburg's comments is not that he is citing an anti-affirmative action scholar known for his conservative views. It is that he suggests that Sowell's work provides conclusive evidence and enough reason that affirmative action must be abandoned. There are many case studies where policies of equity and excellence have yielded positive effects. The book *The Shape of the River* by William Bowen and Derek Bok, former vice-chancellors of Princeton and Harvard, offers careful empirical analysis, and presents quantifiable data which shows the positive outcomes of race-based preferential policies in student admissions, including the social benefits of racial diversity in higher education.

Bowen and Bok's book received high praise as a brilliant and scholarly analysis, but also provoked fierce criticism. Critics accused the authors of drawing conclusions aimed at pursuing a liberal agenda. Nonetheless, the fact remains that other studies have also found benefits in racial diversity – for another example, based on an analysis of nearly 200 universities in the United States, the social psychologist Pat Gurin found that students who experienced the most racial and intellectual diversity in and out of their classrooms benefited in terms of both 'learning outcomes' and 'democracy outcomes'.

Clearly, our institutions in South Africa face some challenges in their implementation of equity policies. Yet there are pressing reasons why the quest for equity in our previously divided and unequal society is a moral virtue that we must pursue. Finding the best way to move the equity agenda forward as part of the democratisation of our society will require a much more nuanced debate and respectful dialogue instead of adopting absolutist positions on the issue.

31. We need to learn how it is for others

Cape Times, 18 April 2011

In February 2011, two public figures made controversial statements about coloured people. The first was the television personality Nomakula (Kuli) Roberts, who wrote a column in Sunday World *about the supposed characteristics of 'Cape coloured women',[23] and the second was government spokesperson Jimmy Manyi, who declared that coloured people were 'overconcentrated' in the Western Cape.[24] In this article I sought to show why their remarks were rightly regarded as offensive.*

A VIGOROUS DEBATE has taken place in the media, in academic institutions, and among the general public since *Sunday World* reporter Kuli Roberts's insulting commentary on coloured identity,[25] and Jimmy Manyi's remarks, from the corridors of power,

---

[23] See News24, 'Kuli's coloured column sparks outrage', 28 February 2011, http://www.news24.com/SouthAfrica/News/Kulis-coloured-column-sparks-outrage-20110228; 'Here's the Kuli Roberts racist article causing all the drama', 28 February 2011, http://lifeissavage.com/2011/02/28/heres-the-kuli-roberts-racist-article-causing-all-the-drama/. In response, *Sunday World* announced that Roberts's column would be discontinued. See *Mail & Guardian*, 'Weekly Kuli Roberts column to be discontinued', 28 February 2011, http://mg.co.za/article/2011-02-28-weekly-kuli-roberts-column-to-be-discontinued.

[24] Manyi made his remark during a TV interview the previous year while he was still director-general of labour, but it only attracted public attention when, in February 2011, extracts from the interview were posted on YouTube by the conservative trade union Solidarity. See *City Press*, 'Manyi under fire for "coloured" remarks', 24 February 2011, http://www.citypress.co.za/politics/manyi-under-fire-for-coloured-remarks-20110224-3/. The ANC distanced itself from his comments, and Manyi eventually issued an apology. See *Mail & Guardian*, 'ANC takes issue with "disturbing" Manyi comments', 25 February, http://mg.co.za/article/2011-02-25-anc-takes-issue-with-disturbing-manyi-comments.

[25] I am a member of the generation of South Africans who were part of the Black Consciousness Movement, and subscribed to its principles and values. Therefore, my preference is to use 'black' to include all South Africans who were

about the 'overconcentration' of coloured people in the Western Cape. Some have invoked 'freedom of speech' to defend the authors over statements that have caused pain among many coloured people. On the other side of the debate, the protagonists of this national drama have been accused of racism.

Neither the human rights lens (freedom of expression) nor the race debate shine the light on what is at the heart of the problem: the continuing exclusion of people from groups that are different from one's own, and treating them as 'the Other'. The effect is a lack of recognition of the worth and dignity of those perceived as the Other, and the ease with which they are denigrated and stripped of their identity as members of the human family. Thus it becomes easy to use words that one normally applies to cattle and inanimate things like stock that may be in high or low supply.

What is frightening about this notion of the 'oversupply' of coloureds is that it conjures up images of slavery, and a time when human life was measured not in terms of its value in social relationships, but rather as mere instruments for fulfilling the demands of production. Considering that slavery is part of the history of the Western Cape, it is not inconceivable that slave masters in this province may have pondered the question of the 'oversupply' of slaves, and considered moving them around to 'balance' the numbers. The apartheid government deliberated on these very same issues, and perfected the plan of controlling black numbers in the cities through influx control policies. Many of us feel sad and disillusioned that language which harkens back to the days of slavery and apartheid is being re-established to frame debates about legislation today.

---

discriminated against by apartheid policies because of their race. The use of the designation 'coloured' in South Africa, however, does have its place: it is pragmatic, in that it is difficult to redress apartheid's legacy without resorting to the language of racial categories; and also symbolic, in that it affirms the identity and history of a particular group of people.

What is missing in the discourse that has been introduced by Manyi is reflective engagement with the past, and an understanding of the strategy of 'preferential treatment' of coloureds in the Western Cape as a policy that was rooted in the apartheid government's divide and rule policy. This is why I believe invoking Steve Biko and the days of Black Consciousness (BC), as some have done, brings this historical past of the apartheid government's social engineering into sharp focus.

During the days of the Black Consciousness Movement (BCM), the designation 'black' was embraced by many black people in all their diversity, because it represented the shared identity and aspirations of people who were marginalised and oppressed under apartheid. The inclusive language was an important cornerstone for the BCM. It eschewed the apartheid government's lines of division among blacks in the interest of higher ideals: black solidarity, and a unified resistance movement against apartheid.

It was an act of defiance among many coloured people who led or joined the struggle for liberation that they refused to be co-opted into the apartheid government's grand scheme of divide and conquer. The result was a more unified front of black activism that transcended the apartheid government's racial and ethnic divisions. Thus, there is some truth in the rallying cry that we have seen in some of the articles and letters to newspaper editors in response to Manyi and Roberts, that their statements about coloured people disrupt the unified narrative of blackness from the BC days. (Interestingly, Biko, in affirming this unity among blacks, pointed out that black people 'have had enough experience as objects of racism not to wish to turn the tables'.)

There is, however, a part of the history of the BCM that has far greater significance for our country today than this story of unity among the oppressed groups under apartheid. Important as it is for getting a perspective in the current debate, the focus on the black unity dimension of the BCM moves us further away from conversations about the humanising principles espoused by Biko and his comrades in the leadership of the BCM throughout the 1970s, principles that lay a foundation for the non-racial politics of the 1980s. The centrality of compassion and care in Biko's message is captured in his vision of a shared humanity, what he called 'the quest for true humanity'. This message of shared humanity in our new South Africa was part of the discourse of the Truth and Reconciliation Commission. It has been quickly abandoned by our leaders in government today, and it is almost non-existent in their public statements.

Biko's profoundly simple yet powerful message calls us to return to the very essence of what it means to be human, to embrace a new consciousness, one based on an ethics of care and compassion for our fellow South Africans. We saw how this wave of true humanity carried the liberation struggle from the 1970s in its focus on a range of programmes designed to build a sense of responsibility among its members for the broader communities within which they lived and beyond.

This spirit of humanity was carried into the 1980s, and it shaped the non-racialism of political struggle throughout that turbulent decade. In the darkest moments in Cape Town, when the fires were burning in KTC and Crossroads, and the South African Defence Force was destroying lives and homes in black townships, the only healing light was in the coloured suburbs. By 'light' I do not mean street lights; I am referring to hundreds of candle lights that lined the streets of coloured suburbs, and collection centres created in these suburbs for clothes and food. It was an expression of solidarity with fellow human beings across the 'geographic' divides created by apartheid.

The resurgence of the human spirit was seen in other parts of Cape Town as well. It is a story, along with the suffering and destruction witnessed in Cape Town in recent apartheid history, that is commemorated in the permanent memorial at the St George's Cathedral's Crypt Memory and Witness Centre. It is testimony not only to the human destruction of the apartheid era, but also, and perhaps more importantly, to the human moments that give us hope in the face of despair.

There has been much despair in recent years because of the apparent impunity with which some in positions of leadership in the ANC have made public statements. Sometimes the utter lack of care for the human dignity of others in these utterances has caused one to cringe with shame. It is worth noting, for a little perspective, that beginning with the period around ANC campaigns to have charges against President Zuma dropped, people in positions of leadership within the ANC or its alliance partners have made a series of troubling, inappropriate, or tasteless statements. Some of these statements, such as 'killing' for Zuma, and calling opponents 'cockroaches' or 'snakes', have been given legitimacy by the ANC leadership in different ways, the most common being that the statements were supposedly only used 'euphemistically'. But I digress – let me return to the statements that motivated me to write this article.

Our country prides itself on having a constitution with a Bill of Rights that is one of the most comprehensive of its kind. Given our political history, and the dehumanising aspects of the apartheid past, respect for human dignity is a core principle of our constitution. The comments by Manyi as a state representative – the very state that is supposed to 'respect, protect, promote and fulfil the rights in the Bill of Rights' – and his flagrant indifference to the hurt he has caused, remind us that we cannot talk about respect

149

for human dignity without a profound understanding of what the essence of human values are. The dignity and worth of all individuals and groups impose an obligation on all of us to practice care and compassion towards others. This requires that we 'see' ourselves in the Other, that is, a reciprocal mutual recognition – recognising the humanity of the Other as much as we would like them to recognise ours.

This, I believe, is the orientation we need to build a spirit of concern for the dignity of others, and a shared humanity into the future of our country. When Manyi says that coloureds are in 'oversupply', whatever the context, those words inflict a wound in many of us. In my case, he is talking about my brother Luyanda's two boys, my sister Nombeko's daughter, my son's friend Mikhail, my friends Bev and Al, and many others. Manyi should consider that he may have to answer for his statements to his grandchildren. In our plural society, his son or daughter may one day announce that they are marrying a partner from a different racial group to his own.

If our face is reflected in the face of the Other, and we are focused on connecting with the Other as a fellow human being rather than as irredeemably Other (coloured, Indian, white, or black African), then we have a better chance of transcending ourselves in order to reach out to others with compassion. In this context, the idea of one's child being of a different race is an evocative one because it invites us to seriously consider the possibility that we might respond to the suffering of the Other as if the Other were our own flesh and blood.

This possibility of shared humanity with others is captured in the words of Biko: 'We have set out on a quest for true humanity, and somewhere on the distant horizon we can see the glittering prize. Let us march forth with courage and determination, drawing strength from our common plight and our brotherhood. In time we shall be in a position to bestow upon South Africa the greatest gift possible – a more human face.'

The guiding principles of Biko's vision are based on a morality that is Other-directed, concerned with promoting the ethical vision of compassion and care for others. By locating the responsibility for a more caring and humane society in ourselves, Biko seems to be calling us to respond not with the force of righteous entitlement to 'freedom of speech' but with the moral force of compassion and care for others. Biko's words point us toward understanding the debate that has erupted about coloured fellow South Africans as a site for ethical engagement, a site for forging human links across time and space with the Other.

WOMEN AND MALE POWER

'After the wars are over, how can governments ensure the protection of women from the silent bombs of male power in their homes and their communities?'

32. Black male chauvinists

MAIL & GUARDIAN, 30 SEPTEMBER 1995

> *On 8 September 1995, Mamphela Ramphele paid tribute to Steve Biko on the 18ᵗʰ anniversary of his death while he was in police custody.[26] In a response published a week later, Professor Itumeleng Mosala, vice-chancellor of Technikon North West and a former Azapo president, unleashed a barrage of personal insults,[27] accusing Ramphele of seeking to appropriate Biko's name and philosophy as a means of climbing the ladder of white privilege. It seemed clear from the tone and language of his article that Ramphele's gender rather than the substance of her arguments was at stake.*

PROFESSOR ITUMELENG MOSALA neither addresses the real issues that Dr Mamphela Ramphele raises, nor does he explain what the philosophy of the Azanian Students' Movement (Azasm) actually is. Instead, he sinks to a depth so base that one struggles to associate the text with the dignity of an academic institution.

There are two main reasons why his response is so depressing. The first is that his rhetoric is underpinned by fantasies of male domination. The second is that it reflects the ironies of the new-found experience of sharing the benefits of equal opportunity. The former attitude is generic among male chauvinists. The latter is peculiar to the black (the pre-1994 meaning of 'black') middle classes in academia and in the corporate world. I will deal with these two issues separately.

---

[26] Mamphela Ramphele, 'Can the dead act as arbitrators', *Mail & Guardian*, 8 September 1995, http://mg.co.za/article/1995-09-08-can-the-dead-act-as-arbitrators.

[27] Itumeleng Mosala, 'A poor tribute', *Mail & Guardian*, 15 September 1995, http://mg.co.za/article/1995-09-15-a-poor-tribute.

Hard-working women in most parts of the world have to face the challenge of male chauvinists, who do not want to take them seriously. Usually, the issue is not about doubting these women's potential. On the contrary, it is precisely the fact that they are competent and have consistently proved superb excellence in tackling every task placed before them.

The frustration felt by the male chauvinist is often couched in words and symbols that claim allegiance to the social order, or 'the culture'. The reality of the matter is this: women, like children, in line with the 'cultural conservatism' of 'our' people, are not supposed to be heard. What kind of *uhuru* is it if the exercise of the right to stand up and publicly express our beliefs means that we are leaving ourselves exposed to potential abuse? If Mosala is a good example of the African male intelligentsia which he lays claim to, his article raises serious doubts about the quality of 'African intelligentsia' in general. His preparedness to compromise his dignity in public is also a poor representation of African male intelligentsia.

The significance of Mosala's obvious anger should be assessed more carefully. A close look at Ramphele's actual statement makes this easy. Clearly, Mosala is still silent about a much more fundamental matter: his problem with a woman who outshines him. Furthermore, he is obviously not speaking for the nation, whose leadership he claims to hold.

So what strategy does he use? What does a black male chauvinist do to rally support among fellow blacks, including women, against a black woman seen as a threat 'to the nation'? He invokes the notion of 'we-ness'. He casts himself in the role of a 'custodian of culture'. Finally, he attributes to himself the characteristic of the prototype of blackness, and claims knowledge of what all black people want.

Black intellectual male chauvinists are perhaps lucky, because they have this tactic available to them. What some people may not recognise is that this is a manipulative stunt that satisfies male chauvinist narcissism. Its aim is to place power and domination where their egos want it: in the hands of men.

Cornel West aptly captures the significance of this issue in his contribution to the book *Race-ing Justice, En-gendering Power* (Pantheon, 1992).[28] In his chapter on 'Black leadership and the pitfalls of racial reasoning', West argues that black nationalist sentiments promote and encourage black cultural conservatism, 'especially black patriarchal power'. He goes on to state: 'The claims to black authenticity that feed on the closing-ranks mentality of black people are dangerous precisely because this closing ranks is usually done at the expense of black women.'[29] Thus the blacker-than-thou (and sometimes whiter-than-I) argument, and the more-in-touch-with-roots claim, are invoked less with 'the community' in mind than as an expression of anxiety about lost power – 'lost' to a woman.

The final point I want to make is about the ironies of equal opportunity. It is a well-known fact that black people in previously white institutions are there because of the principle of equal opportunity adopted by those institutions. I say this with caution. I think it is beside the point whether the appointment of candidates is partly influenced by their blackness. The main challenge is what a person does after the door of equal opportunity has been opened to her or him.

There are several roles that emerge in these institutions. One that puzzles me the most is when black people target another black

---

[28]   Cornel West, 'Black leadership and the pitfalls of racial reasoning', in Toni Morrison (ed.), *Race-ing Justice, En-gendering Power: Essays on Anita Hill, Clarence Thomas, and the Construction of Social Reality*, New York: Pantheon, 1992.

[29]   Ibid, p 395.

person, or more than one, as the source of their frustrations. They spend much of their energy disparaging the contribution of those they perceive as having 'sold out to whites'.

This perception, and the circumstances that produce it, need examination. The way it is used, particularly in the changing power relations in academic institutions, should be carefully evaluated. It is a stifling notion, and one that clouds clear principle and focus. Once this 'other black' is projected as the person responsible for all sorts of failures, very little energy – or none at all – is expended on finding out what the factual situation is. It is enough to say that the person is not black enough.

After reading Mosala's article, I recalled West's comment that black freedom is not a matter of skin pigmentation, but a matter of 'ethical principles and wise politics'. I think it is time for those who make claims to black leadership to set the tone for more meaningful debates, particularly in places of higher learning.

33. When choice is not an option

ThisDay, 2 April 2004

> *At an election rally in March 2004, President Thabo Mbeki remarked in isiXhosa that he would beat his sister if she told him she was in love with Reverend Kenneth Meshoe, leader of the African Christian Democratic Party. Although the crowd interpreted this as a humorous remark, I felt it reflected something of the casual normalisation of violence against women.[30]*

PRESIDENT THABO MBEKI'S reportedly jocular remark during an election rally about beating his sister was reckless. Why is it that at one of the very rare occasions when we hear the president speaking publicly about an issue that affects many women – violence – it is as a joke? How can an experience that is real and painful for millions of South African women be made into a joke by the head of state? In a society where the rate of domestic abuse and rape is counted among the worst in the world, where the beating of women by their fathers, brothers, husbands and lovers is no laughing matter, how can the president joke about this?

It sends the wrong signal to women and men who are working hard to change sexist language, perceptions and attitudes that contribute to the normalisation of violence against women. The president's statement not only legitimises the treatment of women as objects, but perpetuates the stereotype of men – African men – as violent, sexual, sexist beings who want to control and dominate women, and who, if women are unwilling to acquiesce,

---

[30] See T Butcher, 'Women enraged by Mbeki gaffe', *The Telegraph*, 24 March 2004; 'Mbeki "only joking"', News24 Online, 22 March 2004; 'Mbeki under fire for sister gaffe', BBC News, 23 March 2004.

WOMEN AND MALE POWER

will physically punish them. It raises many questions not only about the messages communicated at leadership level about gender issues, but also whether we can relax now that we have a non-sexist constitution and gender-sensitive policies.

The remark resonates far beyond the election campaign. The images of sex and violence that it reflects touch women in one of the most vulnerable aspects of their lives at present: sexual autonomy. When it comes to making choices in sexual relationships, the majority of women have no voice, no power. The recent finding by the South African Medical Research Council that more women than men are dying of AIDS reminds us of how far-reaching this state of affairs is. Many HIV/AIDS intervention programmes are based simply on the prevention element of condoms, while the caregiving aspects focus only on counselling and treatment. The issue of male social power and gender dynamics, so crudely captured by Mbeki's fundamentally sexist remark, is rarely considered.

Last week, I spent Human Rights Day in KTC, a township near Cape Town, speaking with women living with HIV/AIDS. The theme of the conversations was that of helplessness, not only in relation to condom use, but also regarding making decisions about whether to stay in a relationship where the risk of HIV infection is high.

'When he started sleeping around early in our relationship, I tried to leave him,' said one very young woman referring to her partner. 'But he would beat me blue, accusing me of having an affair.' One day she returned from the clinic and told him about the HIV-positive results of her blood test. He beat her up, saying the results confirmed his suspicions about her seeing another man, and left. 'Now it's too late,' she said after a long silence, placing her hand protectively on her pregnant stomach. She turned away from me to look out through the door of the tiny tin home where she lives with her mother.

Clearly, since HIV/AIDS develops in a context of social inequality, it is a human rights issue. Women who are at risk of HIV infection face multiple victimisation – simply by being women. Their right to make choices that could reduce the chances of being infected is taken away by a culture that privileges men, and forces women into the silence of submission.

The 'weaker' sex is further weakened by their poor socio-economic circumstances which predisposes them to dependency and renders them unable to leave emotionally and physically abusive relationships. Not only women's biological make-up makes them vulnerable to HIV infection, but also their powerlessness to question partners about their extramarital affairs, refuse to have sex with unfaithful partners, or negotiate the introduction of condoms. They are disadvantaged by the socio-cultural context that equates men's multiple sexual encounters with masculinity.

HIV prevention strategies will only succeed if these factors are taken into account. Programmes ought to incorporate an empowerment and skills training plan for women from low socio-economic areas. Where the risk of HIV infection is high, not only economic empowerment for women is needed, but also partnerships with men and the incorporation of a human rights agenda for women in intervention programmes.

In this time of HIV/AIDS crisis, policy documents alone cannot forge our democracy. We may have some of the best laws and policies that affect gender power relations, but the evil of sexism is not only about equal access to opportunities for men and women. It is also about the position of women in a cultural context. For certain groups of women, gender relations affect their ability to make choices that will protect them from HIV infection.

One of the surest ways of changing risky forms of behaviour – such as multiple partners and unprotected sex – is a rigorous 'informational cascade' where leaders use election campaigns to instil values like compassion, dignity, and responsible sex.

34. The tears of Sierra Leone

CAPE TIMES, 8 MARCH 2006

> *In 2006 I travelled to Sierra Leone on a United Nations Development Fund for Women (UNIFEM) assignment, spending 18 days speaking to women who had survived the horrific civil war. I wrote this article shortly after my return.*

LUNSAR, SIERRA LEONE: Isatu Bangura[31] can hardly control her tears as she describes the morning when her parents were forced to watch her being gang-raped by rebels. They shot her mother first. One of the soldiers pushed the butt of his gun under her father's chin, telling him to 'chin up' for a 'bonus memory'. She was raped again by two of the men, while the others shot her father. The rebels then forced Isatu to carry loads of looted goods, driving her to the bush, where she was used as a sex slave until she escaped three years later. She was 13 years old.

It is 40° degrees Celsius inside the small office of a women's skills centre run by Fatmata Kobba. In the corner of the room, Nemata, a young mother, breaks into uncontrollable sobs. Distraught, she tries to wipe away her tears with the back of her hand. On her lap she holds a tiny baby, and she is expecting another child. Already a mother of two at 16, she is too young to be a mother at all. Her children's father was her captor, and his comrades had shot her parents in front of her before cutting off her older brother's hands with machetes because he had refused to obey their orders to rape her. There are 13 women in the room, all listening silently with collective sorrow in their eyes.

When one thinks of Sierra Leone, images of the indescribable war that knew no bounds spring to mind. I am in Lunsar, two

---

[31] Not her real name.

hours north from Freetown, the capital city, talking to women who bear heart-rending emotional and physical scars from the country's decade-long war.

The years 1991 and 1992 in Sierra Leone marked the beginning of the ruthless attacks by the Revolutionary United Front (RUF). They attacked the poorest and most helpless, dubbing their atrocities names like 'Operation Fine Girl' and 'Operation No Living Thing.' They raped, murdered, indiscriminately slicing off women's breasts and their husbands' genitals, chopping off the hands and feet of adults, children, and sometimes infants, and slashed pregnant women's stomachs with machetes. To be visibly pregnant was to know death. Rebels were known to play a betting game on the gender of the foetus before slashing a woman's stomach open to find out who had won the bet.

Many of the young men who wreaked murderous rebellion in the civilian population were boys who were forced to kill their parents as a form of initiation. To make the boy-soldiers 'brave', rebel commanders and their aides would make an incision on the forehead of a boy-soldier and fill it with cocaine.

I saw these crude and frightful scars on the faces of some of the young men on the streets of Freetown, and I found I could not help the images that streamed through my mind, drawn from the horrific experiences described by the women I had met. I wondered which one of the young men had been little boys in oversized army camouflage uniforms wielding their oversized weapons, and whether any of them were tormented by what they had done and witnessed.

Freetown is a city holding its breath. There is something surreal about driving in the city, as if I'm walking through a film about the destruction that befell the people of Sierra Leone. The hollow structures of blackened burnt buildings are visible around the city and all along the road to the northern part of the country, against the backdrop of beautiful rivers and the majestic hills and mountains that earned Sierra Leone its name of 'Lion Mountain'.

Now four years since the war was declared officially over, the signature of the rebels is not only visible in the ruins of the once elegant hotels and homes, but also in the limbless men, women, and children one sees in the streets. Passing some of the armless and legless Sierra Leoneans in the streets of Freetown who were cruelly 'amputated' by the rebels is a painful reminder of how evil can so easily emerge and thrive among human beings.

Rape as a weapon of war in Sierra Leone has had devastating effects on the lives of women and girls. With more than 500 000 women reported to have suffered rape, and many forced to become sex slaves, many women continue to live with the physical scars of multiple long-term rape, notably the condition known as vesico-vaginal fistula (VVF), namely the development of an abnormal tract between a woman's bladder and her vagina, resulting in a continuous leak of urine.

A group of women who wake up every day to set up their stalls in the open market in Freetown shared sorrowful experiences of the shame and anxiety they face daily, not knowing when they will lose control of their bladders. The tragedy is that their harrowing experiences have left them worse off than they were before the war.

'My parents were killed. All I have is the man who had captured me and made me his wife. I have all these children from him, what can I do?' said Nemata, who lives with the former RUF rebel who abducted her during the war.

This reality of choiceless choices is hauntingly echoed in the experience of Isatu Bangura: 'After the war I became a prostitute. I'm back in my village now to take a break from the darkness in my life. I thought to myself, well, my mother is dead, my father is dead.

Nobody to tell me what to do now. I'm all alone in the world. ... The rebels used us for nothing. But now at least we are paid for our sex. We are just consoling ourselves. But where can we go?'

The ruins and devastation of the merciless havoc wreaked by the rebels in Sierra Leone extend far beyond the buildings that they destroyed. The cycle of violence and orgy of terror against society's weakest and most helpless – women – continues to play itself out in domestic violence, the sexual abuse of young girls, and the high rate of rape of women and girls.

On a continent where countless numbers of women and girls have been victims of war rape, there is no 'post conflict' for women. For many women on the continent, the silent time bomb that waits ominously is male power, wielded by some men through their sex organs. The Zuma trial that reopened this week in Johannesburg is a poignant reminder of this fact.

Binta Yema's parents were killed execution-style before the rebels abducted her when she was 11. Now 21, she sits quietly working on her batik cloth in the skills centre, imagining the horror of her evening when she goes home to her uncle's house: 'I know he is going to use me [rape me],' she says absent-mindedly; 'it's like that every night.'

Today is International Women's Day, and an excellent opportunity to reflect on the question: after the wars are over, how can governments ensure the protection of women from the silent bombs of male power in their homes and their communities?

35. Daughter of Africa, go to rest in peace

SUNDAY TIMES, 23 APRIL 2006

In this article, I paid tribute to an extraordinary South African, Ellen Kuzwayo – pioneering social worker, political activist and women's rights activist – shortly after her death at age 91.

'THE STORY OF my life, my education, you see, cannot be buried quietly and safely in the past. How can I remain quiet when I see the choices open to the younger generation constantly restricted, their hopes fading into dreams, and their dreams becoming nightmares?'

These are the words of Mama Ellen Kuzwayo, immortalised in her autobiography *Call Me Woman*,[32] and in the memories of the thousands of people whose lives she touched, including mine. They are strong words that simultaneously confront and haunt – confront us with the silence of her death, and haunt us with the truth that they foretold.

With the passing of Ellen Kuzwayo, South Africa has lost one of its crusaders for the liberation of women through the struggle for change and social justice. Her star shines brightly in our hearts. We mourn her death, and we celebrate her story, which she told with such eloquent grace, and lived with dignity, courage and compassion through the most volatile times of our country's history until her final days.

The hallmark of Ellen Kuzwayo's genius is the simple things, which are surprisingly hard to come by these days: a strong sense of community and compassion, and an abiding love of justice.

---

[32] Ellen Kuzwayo, *Call Me Woman*, London: The Women's Press, 1985. Reprinted by Aunt Lute Books, 1992.

165

Her life was so profoundly political because she shared it so readily with others. Those values deeply shaped her life, a life that will continue to inspire with its richness in spite of its heritage of suffering, and continue to touch many of us intimately because it was so ordinary.

Kuzwayo was born in 1914, and raised on a farm belonging to her great-grandparents at Thaba Nchu in the Free State. When she speaks of her childhood on the farm in *Call Me Woman*, there is joy and longing in her words: a happy, carefree childhood roaming the vast land and surrounding hills, 'free as a bird'. Her family was later forcibly dispossessed, and the farm sold. The apartheid government had made it illegal for blacks to own land in the area. The spirit of the freedom of Kuzwayo's youth, however, burned in her heart, and she became a courageous champion for women's rights and for the rights of children and families.

'Ma K was a remarkable, brave and incredibly strong woman,' Joyce Seroke tells me. Seroke, now the chairman of the Commission on Gender Equality, attributes many of the important lessons in her life – including her political activism, and returning to university to pursue post-graduate studies – to Ma Kuzwayo. 'She was bold. I learned from her that age is not a barrier to pursuing serious studies.'

Kuzwayo studied for her high school education at Adams College in KwaZulu-Natal and completed her teacher training at Lovedale College in the Eastern Cape. Those schools, as well as the Jan H. Hofmeyr School of Social Work where Kuzwayo later went, were some of the best institutions where blacks could study at the time. Kuzwayo, formidable, determined and unstoppable, added the University of the Witwatersrand to her list of South African institutions of note when, at age 69, she graduated with a Higher Diploma in Social Work.

For those of my generation who studied social work, Ellen Kuzwayo was a shining example of those members of the generation before us whom we wanted to emulate – formidable, erudite, principled women whose values, character and poise inspired us. She will be remembered as one of the women whose deep sense of character and principles paved the way for the next generation, and kept alive the flame of hope that brought us as women to a place where we can speak out in safety.

Pregs Govender, a former ANC member of parliament who famously abstained from voting on the 2001 Defence Budget, spoke to me about Kuzwayo's profound influence on her: 'I have no words to describe what a deep inspiration she was,' Govender said. 'Her constant encouragement for our work on the Women's Budget process was legendary.'

Kuzwayo's spirit of generous support and caring for other women extended far beyond the walls of parliament, where she served with the first democratically elected government in 1994. Leah Tutu, wife of Archbishop Desmond Tutu, described this quality as one of her most remarkable ones: 'She had her feet firmly on the ground, and so was able to reach out to people from all walks of life. She had a strong sense of community, and a great sense of family life – she adored her sons,' Tutu said.

Perhaps it was the strength of Kuzwayo's commitment to her family that made her so unique as a political activist. Her experiences as a black woman under apartheid, and her struggles in her first marriage, painfully described in *Call Me Woman*, probably gave her a greater capacity for compassion with many women who live in fear in their own homes.

Her life is a story of great suffering, yet – as close friends and colleagues like Joyce Seroke describe her – it is also a portrait of the love she shared with her second husband, Godfrey Kuzwayo, of a profoundly beautiful person, and of an elegant and deeply feminine woman who loved life. She defended her life – by leaving an abusive husband, defying the system of apartheid, and protecting the lives of those who were voiceless and in need of care. That she was able to feel the deepest compassion for other women, and those in need, is the remarkable legacy of many women who have known suffering.

There was a memorable moment when Kuzwayo appeared before the Truth and Reconciliation Commission at a special hearing about the events in Soweto in June 1976. She described the brutal drama of the killing of pupils, and sketched the depravity among the youth she had observed over the years since the tragic events of June 16. Then she lamented the irreparable loss of self-respect and respect for others that she had witnessed among young people: 'I am still angry because the Nationalist government never saw our children as children,' she said. 'We talk about violence in this country, violence that is carried out by young people – they turned our children into animals. I think I will go to my grave with this pain in my heart.'

Many women share the anguish that other women face in their homes, their communities and their workplaces; the loss of their children, including loss through violent crime, whether as victims or perpetrators. These problems remain, as they did for Kuzwayo, a source of pain in our hearts, perhaps even a potent source of bitterness and hate. They may, however, also be a compelling reason for us to – just for a moment – let go of the bitterness, and instead celebrate the memory of Ma Kuzwayo, and acknowledge the debt we owe to the continuation of her life's work.

Towards the end of her book, she summoned all the women who had touched her life, in whose footsteps she had followed, women who had given her the gift of love, strength, character and strong values. Then she filled the remaining pages with celebration. To each of these women, she bade a special farewell.

Here too, I bid you, Mama Kuzwayo, this farewell: 'Go to rest in peace, Daughter of Africa. You have served your nation and your country. You have inspired us and made us.'

36. Keeping the spirit of 1956 alive

MAIL & GUARDIAN, 4 AUGUST 2006

The groundswell of support for Jacob Zuma during his rape trial in the Johannesburg High Court was staggering. Zuma supporters outside the courtroom chanted 'Burn this bitch' while holding up images of the complainant, as well as a poster saying, 'How much did they pay you, nondindwa [bitch]?'[33] This article was my response.

IN HER PREFACE to Karina Turok's book *Life and Soul: Portraits of Women Who Move South Africa*,[34] Mamphela Ramphele celebrates the strength of women, their resilience and resolve in the face of adversity. Echoing an earlier period of women's struggle – in this case, against the hated pass laws – Ramphele reminds us of the resolute spirit that inspired 20 000 women to march to the Union Buildings on 9 August 1956 in a direct challenge to apartheid oppression.

As we celebrate the 50th anniversary of that fearless march, we are humbled by the memory of how South African women took a bold step to become the makers of history. The legendary phrase that captures the force and spirit of that historic event sums it up for me: '*Wathint'abafazi; wathint'imbokotho*' (You have struck women; you have struck a rock).

Drawing strength from the momentum created five decades ago by women who united across class and racial lines, many South African women have carried the torch forward and distinguished themselves in business, government, religious institutions,

---

[33] *Mail & Guardian*, 'Timeline of the Jacob Zuma rape trial', 21 March 2006, http://mg.co.za/article/2006-03-21-timeline-of-the-jacob-zuma-rape-trial.

[34] Karina Turok, *Life and Soul: Portraits of Women Who Move South Africa*, Cape Town: Double Storey, 2009.

academia, and community organisations. Standing tall, strong and talented, women are today visible at the highest levels of leadership in several sectors of society – and there are many more on the horizon, poised to lead with the same fearlessness and spirit of resolve witnessed 50 years ago on the steps of the Union Buildings.

The successes of women who have achieved in life are visible everywhere: in parliament, in local government, in non-governmental organisations and in business. As part of celebrating Women's Day, local magazines have given us a good sense of the strength and visibility of women who are trailblazers in various corporate organisations. These women's stories are celebrated as examples of how far we have come. They make us proud.

Yet there is another group of women who remain largely unacknowledged. The tradition of the courageous spirit of women continues to live through the stories of ordinary women whose visibility is confined to the communities they serve. These are the women in the 'trenches' of South African rural and urban areas who face the day-to-day struggles of poverty, HIV/AIDS, crime and insecurity, and sexual violence against themselves and their children. These are women who have formed a grassroots movement of social supports – creating livelihoods, caring for others, giving support, and trying to build a sense of safety in their communities. These women, every day, are keeping the spirit of 1956 alive.

The struggle for respect, freedom and dignity that brought women to Pretoria half a century ago was a struggle against apartheid. In the 50 years since then, women, wherever they are, have made huge advances. Our constitution, as well as the leadership of President Thabo Mbeki, is strong on issues of gender equality. Women continue, as they must, to mobilise, to gain strength in their networks, and to fight for equality and against injustice. The enemy, however, is no longer apartheid. The enemy is an old system that unites women across colour and class lines – the system of patriarchy. The growing change in gender dynamics and the courageous manner in which women are increasingly making their voices heard is challenging those who want to preserve this social relic.

In recent months, no event illustrated this problem like the Jacob Zuma rape trial, which focused our thoughts sharply on the issue of patriarchy. A chorus of voices from the leadership of the Congress of South African Trade Unions (COSATU), the ANC Youth League and the Young Communist League during the trial seemed to negate all that we have achieved in the past half-century. The attitudes about women revealed in the tenor of their comments – including from those who aspire to become leaders of the ANC – are frightening.

Ramphele refers to the tension between the desire to pursue gender equality and men's fears about this agenda. That debate continues today. 'Women legislators are being harassed by fellow legislators [who are] custodians of our constitution,' she writes. 'That tells me that the job we needed to do during the struggle is not complete.'

Women need a platform to continue the struggle. Perhaps the South African Women in Dialogue, initiated by Zanele Mbeki, could provide a platform for us to create a shared vision and a strategy to address the problems that continue to stifle development on the gender equality front. Some of these problems are due to the attitudes and behaviours of men. The questions of how to deal with these obstacles should be part of an ongoing dialogue between men and women.

The gains of our constitution, made visible through various laws, gender committees and gender desks, will not advance the cause of women in the long term if the ideology of patriarchy remains intact. Dialogue is a vital tool that is necessary for meaningful transformation among men to occur. But dialogue alone may not change the men whose behaviour continues to undermine gender equality: it should be preceded by a visible demonstration of women's strength and unity.

The women's march to the Union Buildings 50 years ago is one of the most inspiring stories of the anti-apartheid movement. It is a story of great victory that marks the beginning of women's transformation. We need another march to renew the fight against an enemy that has been in our midst for too long: patriarchy. This time, women should gather outside the venue of the ANC's next national conference, in 2007, to ensure that those selected to lead the country are committed to the advance of women's equality.

Acknowledgements

I am indebted to my editor at Tafelberg, Kristin Paremoer, her colleagues and the copy-editor, Riaan de Villiers, for transforming the initial compilation of the chapters in this book to its current form. Kristin stayed close to the project throughout, offering different pieces of wisdom along the way. Thank you also to Denis Gray who worked with me on the first effort to compile my writings into book form.

About the author

Pumla Gobodo-Madikizela is a research professor in trauma, memory and forgiveness at the University of the Free State. She was previously Associate professor of Psychology at the University of Cape Town, becoming a full professor in 2010.

Gobodo-Madikizela served on the Truth and Reconciliation Commission as coordinator of victims' public hearings in the Western Cape. This experience led her to write the award-winning book *A Human Being Died That Night*, about her interactions with the infamous apartheid assassin Eugene de Kock. It won the Alan Paton Literary Award, and formed the basis for a play of the same name which played to acclaim in London in 2012 and in South Africa in 2013.

She works with various organisations within South Africa and internationally to facilitate processes of forgiveness, overcoming collective trauma, and reconciliation.